AUTHENTIC SOCIAL JUSTICE

CHRISTOPHER CONE, TH.D, PH.D, PH.D

EXEGETICA PUBLISHING
2020

This book is dedicated to my brothers and sisters who come from different ethnicities, backgrounds, and cultures. May this work be a blessing to you and an expression of the love that we are designed to have for one another.

For we all are of one race,
Created in His image
And for His glory.

Authentic Social Justice

©2020 Christopher Cone

Published by Exegetica Publishing
Independence, Missouri

ISBN – 978-0-9982805-7-8

All Scripture quotations, except those noted otherwise are from the New American Standard Bible, ©1960,1962,1963,1968,1971,1972,1973,1975, 1977, and 1995 by the Lockman Foundation.

TABLE OF CONTENTS

CHAPTER 1: THE ORIGIN OF INDIVIDUAL CIVIL LIBERTIES ... 7

CHAPTER 2: HOW DID WE GET HERE? 31

CHAPTER 3: BIBLICAL SOCIO-POLITICAL FOUNDATIONS...... 43

CHAPTER 4: THREE VIEWS ON THE KINGDOM 77

CHAPTER 5: THREE VIEWS ON LAW AND ETHICS 85

CHAPTER 6: THE ESSENTIAL EQUALITY OF WOMEN (BY CHRISTOPHER AND CATHERINE CONE)......... 97

CHAPTER 7: ADDRESSING LGBTQ: A BIBLICAL TELEOLOGICAL ARGUMENT......... 113

CHAPTER 8: EVERY TRIBE, TONGUE, PEOPLE, AND NATION 139

CHAPTER 9: THE INSUFFICIENCY OF CRITICAL RACE THEORY 175

CHAPTER 10: IS CHRISTIANITY BAD FOR THE ENVIRONMENT? 185

CHAPTER 11: GRACE IN POLITICS 197

CHAPTER 1
THE ORIGIN OF INDIVIDUAL CIVIL LIBERTIES[1]

The Declaration of Independence makes the audacious claim that "all men are created equal ... endowed by their Creator with certain unalienable rights." This assertion of origin is rooted in a Judeo-Christian worldview – or more precisely, a Biblical one – and has been embraced by America's founding fathers and their philosophical progenitors. In contrast, Plato's ideal of Republic and its implementation in contemporary Marxist theory is rooted in an opposing understanding of the origin and scope of human rights. These two competing socio-political systems underscore the significance of human origin for practical aspects of societal structures and daily life within those constructs.

This paper examines the Biblical roots of individual civil liberties, showing the importance of interpretive method applied to key passages. In literal grammatical historical renderings, the Declaration's unalienable rights claim is affirmed, while other hermeneutic devices allow for an ecclesiastic advocacy of

---

[1] Originally presented to the Council on Dispensational Hermeneutics as "The Biblical Origin of Individual Civil Liberties and Two Competing Views on Their Legitimacy and Implementation," September 16, 2020.

the Platonic/Marxian alternative. Either system can be championed in the name of God, depending on the hermeneutic employed. This is, in the pursuit of a proper worldview, another key instance in which the importance of interpretive method is discernible, and dispensational conclusions can be seen as having much greater (positive) reach than has been traditionally assumed by their critics.

PLATO'S PHILOSOPHER KING IDEAL
VERSUS THE GENESIS-REVELATION DOXOLOGY

Plato (428-348BC) asserts that the human *psuche* is comprised of three parts: appetite, spirit, and mind. The appetite represents the basic desires, and that which might ground an artisan to pursue his craft in order to meet those basic needs. Spirit is the passion that would drive a person toward justice and protection. The mind is that which undergirds a reflective and thoughtful approach to life. Each individual possesses all three elements, but one will dominate. If a person is primarily driven by appetite, that person will (and should) be an artisan – one of the business class. If a person is directed by spirit, that person would be well fitted to be a guardian – one of the military class – in order to help protect society. If a person is more shaped by mind, that person may be well fitted to be at the top of the guardian class as a philosopher king. It is only the enlightened mind-centrics who are qualified to lead society in this way. Because artisans and lower guardians have very limited perspectives and are not predisposed to examine life and understand how it all works, the philosopher kings are the necessary rulers of society. Only they have the needed enlightenment to rightly govern and direct society. For society to flourish, the "organ of knowledge must be turned around from the world of becoming...until the soul is able to endure the contemplation of essence and the brightest region of being."[2] Only the philosopher kings were able to accomplish this correct understanding of reality. For Plato, then, there was little concern for individual rights – particularly in the oversight of society. His priority was the well-being of the Republic, and that could only be ensured when the philosopher kings were ruling. It is based on this metaphysical understanding that Plato despised democracy, for democracy represented a rule by those who were unenlightened and could not possibly govern well. Plato's anthropocentric, naturalistic elitism is a direct antithesis to Biblical conceptions of government and rule.

Genesis 1:26-27 records God's decree for the creation of humanity and the fulfilling of the decree. Unlike any other aspect of creation, the man and woman were created in the image of God,[3] and thus possessed the qualification and the qualities needed to govern His world as He prescribed.[4] It is evident that those qualifications and qualities were at least altered if not destroyed at the Fall,[5] leaving behind a human race imprinted with the image of Adam[6] – broken and separated from God. This new reality for humanity was one of fallenness and incapacity to fulfill the rule and subdue mandate. The mandate was redacted, or rescinded, and humanity was no longer expected to govern as initially prescribed (hence the

---

[2] Plato, *The Republic Books VI-X*, Paul Shorey, trans. (Cambridge, MA: Harvard University Press, 1935), (518c), 135.
[3] Genesis 1:27.
[4] Genesis 1:28.
[5] Genesis 2:17.
[6] Genesis 5:3.

concept of *redacted dominionism*).[7] Still God promised to provide a redemptive path for humanity,[8] and He fulfilled that promise in the person and work of Jesus the Christ.[9] Restoration and reconciliation with God was provided for all through belief in Him.[10]

While the provisions for redemption were put in place, the rule of humanity over creation was not restored. As Paul puts it, "the whole creation groans and suffers the pains of childbirth together until now..."[11] One day when hope is fulfilled, the creation itself will be redeemed at His glorification. Christ Himself will fulfill the human mandate for governance,[12] as He is the only (untarnished) one with the qualifications and qualities to do so. Until the inauguration of His rule, human government is flawed and doomed to failure.[13]

God's redemptive plan for humanity is a central Scriptural theme but is not His highest goal. The redemptive plan serves His doxological purpose – to express His own glory and character.[14] The Bible underscores a redemptive plan for humanity's ultimate restoration, and that plan is designed and executed by God for the purpose of His own glory.

While Plato asserts that only the most enlightened of humanity should rule, and that quality for governance is measured by quality of mind, the Biblical model suggests that human government is inherently imperfect until the qualified

---

[7] Cf., Genesis 1:17-28 and 9:7.
[8] Genesis 3:15, 12:1-3, 15:6, 22:10-18.
[9] Romans 5.
[10] Genesis 15:6, John 3:16, Ephesians 2:8-9.
[11] Romans 8:22.
[12] Revelation 20.
[13] E.g., Daniel 2.
[14] As expressed in Ephesians 1:5,6,12,14.

King takes His throne. Plato's ideal is the philosopher king. The Biblical ideal is the Messianic King. Plato's socio-political system is anthropocentric. The Biblical model is theocentric. It is evident then that a Biblical model for human rights is undergirded by the doxological principle and derives human value not from human achievement, but from Divine design. It is for this foundational reason that the contemporary progressive socialist socio-political tendencies reflect Platonic rather than Scriptural thinking, yet Plato's conclusions are found not only in atheistic elucidations of human rights (such as that of Marx and Engels) but also in some theistic models. It is especially in these cases that hermeneutic inconsistencies lead to socio-political inconsistencies.

FILMER'S ASSERTION OF SCRIPTURAL DIVINE RIGHT

Richard Filmer (1588-1653) describes and opposes a common seventeenth-century view, that "Mankind is naturally endowed and born with Freedom from all Subjection, and at liberty to choose what Form of Government it please: And that the Power which any one Man hath over others, was at first bestowed according to the discretion of the Multitude."[15] He characterizes the view as popularized by divines to minimize the king's authority and facilitate the Church's increasing influence and power.[16] By contrast, Filmer suggests, "the Scripture is not favourable to the Liberty of the People,"[17] that desire for liberty was the cause of Adam's fall and was consequently as dangerous

---

[15] Sir Richard Filmer Baronet, *Patriarcha: Or the Natural Power of Kings* (London: Richard Chiswell, 1680), Chapter 1.
[16] Filmer, 1.1
[17] Filmer, 2.1.

for moderns as it was for Adam.[18] Filmer assigns motive to Adam (desire for liberty), employing a theological hermeneutic, going beyond what is written, and effectively supporting the divine right view by that one supposition. Nothing in the Genesis text nor later texts dare assign motive to Adam. Rather the accounts and later commentary (including nine direct NT references to Adam) simply provide the historical facts of what occurred.

Filmer's hermeneutic maneuver allows him to view authority as imbued in a parental sense. He says, "I see not then how the Children of Adam, or of any man else can be free from subjection to their Parents: And this subjection of Children being the Fountain of all Regal Authority, by the Ordination of God himself; It follows, that Civil Power, not only in general is by Divine Institution, but even the Assignment of it Specifically to the eldest Parents, which quite takes away that New and Common distinction which refers only Power Universal and Absolute to God; but Power Respective in regard of the Special Form of Government to the Choice of the people."[19] Authority, in Filmer's view is through parentage, and it is not a far reach for Filmer to connect parental authority with the authority of the king: "As long as the first Fathers of Families lived, the name of Patriarchs did aptly belong unto them; but after a few Descents, when the true Fatherhood it self was extinct, and only the Right of the Father descends to the true Heir, then the Title of Prince or King was more significant, to express the Power of him who succeeds only to the Right of that Fatherhood which his Ancestors did Naturally enjoy; by this means it comes to pass, that many a Child, by succeeding a King, hath the Right of a

---

[18] Filmer, 1.1.
[19] Filmer, 1.4.

Father over many a Gray-headed Multitude, and hath the Title of Pater Patriæ."[20]

In Filmer's view the king had divine authority to govern as a parent of the people. While in some cases kings were removed or deposed, such was only accomplished by Divine will, even if unrighteous acts (such as rebellion) were employed by the people to accomplish regime change. Filmer asserts that, "If it please God, for the Correction of the Prince, or punishment of the People, to suffer Princes to be removed, and others to be placed in their rooms, either by the Factions of the Nobility, or Rebellion of the People; in all such cases, the Judgment of God, who hath Power to give and to take away Kingdoms, is most just: Yet the Ministry of Men who Execute Gods Judgments without Commission, is sinful and damnable. God doth but use and turn men's Unrighteous Acts to the performance of his Righteous Decrees."[21] This imbued authority was absolute and unconditional, and assured in every generation: "the Authority that is in any one, or in many, or in all these, is the only Right and natural Authority of a Supream Father. There is, and always shall be continued to the end of the World, a Natural Right of a Supreme Father over every Multitude."[22]

Filmer provides no remedy for investable tyranny, as "The Father of a Family governs by no other Law than by his own Will; not by the Laws and Wills of his Sons or Servants. There is no Nation that allows Children any Action or Remedy for being unjustly Governed."[23] Still, natural law demands that the king seek to preserve his people. Thus the interests of the

---

[20] Filmer, 1.8.
[21] Filmer, 1.9.
[22] Filmer, 1.10.
[23] Filmer, 3.1.

many necessarily outweigh those of the individual. The most significant implication of Filmer's divine right theory is that there simply are no individual rights, and Filmer justifies that principle as part of a system for human governance that is built on New Testament (NT) teaching: "If any desire the direction of the New Testament, he may find our Saviour limiting and distinguishing Royal Power, By giving to Cæsar those things that were Cæsar's, and to God those things that were God's...We must obey where the Commandment of God is not hindered; there is no other Law but God's Law to hinder our Obedience."[24] God limits royal power, but does not provide specific ground rules for its expression. There is a wall of separation then between God's sovereignty expressed in the affairs of humanity and the workings of human government, all by virtue of the first hermeneutic device – a theological imputation of motive to Adam.

JOHN LOCKE'S PERSONAL FREEDOM MODEL

John Locke's (1632-1704) model eliminates Filmer's wall altogether, as he directly castigates Filmer's view. Locke says after reading *Patriarcha*, that he was "mightily surprised that in a book, which was to provide chains for all mankind, I should find nothing but a rope of sand."[25] In his first *Treatise* Locke seems bewildered at Filmer's willingness to see all humanity born enslaved, and remarks early in his work that "Slavery is so

---

[24] Filmer, 3.3.
[25] John Locke, Two Treatises on Government (London: Printed for Thomas Tegg; W. Sharpe and Son; G. Offor; G. and J. Robinson; J. Evans and Co.: Also R. Griffin and Co. Glasgow; and J. Gumming, Dublin, 1823), 7.

vile and miserable an estate of man, and so directly opposite to the generous temper and courage of our nation, that it is hardly to be conceived that an Englishman, much less a gentleman, should plead for it."[26]

As Locke critiques Filmer's divine right view, he first takes on Filmer's argument from Adam, summarizing Filmer's case and then lamenting that "the thing is there so taken for granted, without proof, that I could scarce believe myself, when, upon attentive reading that treatise, I found there so mighty a structure raised upon the bare supposition of this foundation."[27] Specifically, Locke challenges Filmer's assertion that Adam's authority was the basis of human government. Locke lambasts Filmer for not proving his assertion, nor even really arguing for it. But by making an assertion "drawn from the authority of Scripture,"[28] Filmer opened himself up to scrutiny for his exegesis. Locke responds as any good hermeneut should: "If he has in that chapter, or any where in the whole treatise, given any other proofs of Adam's royal authority, other than by often repeating it, which, among some men, goes for argument, I desire any body for him to show me the place and page, that I may be convinced of my mistake, and acknowledge my oversight."[29]

Locke further challenges Filmer's assertion that Adam was given governmental authority over humanity at the creation, recounting in some detail the text of Genesis: "First, it is false, that God made that grant to Adam, as soon as he was created, since, though it stands in the text immediately after his

---

[26] Locke, 7.
[27] Locke, 13.
[28] Locke, 14.
[29] Locke 13-14.

creation, yet it is plain it could not be spoken to Adam till after Eve was made and brought to him; and how then could he be monarch by appointment as soon as created, especially since he calls, if I mistake not, that which God says to Eve, Gen. iii. 16, the original grant of government, which not being till after the fall, when Adam was somewhat, at least in time, and very much distant in condition, from his creation, I cannot see, how our [Author, referring to Filmer] can say in this sense, that, "by God's appointment, as soon as Adam was created, he was monarch of the world."[30] Filmer had asserted that Adam had royal authority over all *including humanity.* Locke suggests that there was no element of authority over humanity until – at the earliest, Genesis 3:16. In short, according to Locke, Filmer cannot assert exegetically that Adam had a natural sovereignty over humanity at creation. Locke adds that, "Whatever God gave by the words of this grant Gen. i. 28, it was not to Adam in particular, exclusive of all other men: whatever dominion he had thereby, it was not a private dominion, but a dominion in common with the rest of mankind. That this donation was not made in particular to Adam, appears evidently from the words of the text, it being made to more than one; for it was spoken in the plural number, God blessed them, and said unto them, have dominion."[31]

While Locke says much more against Filmer's assertion of Scriptural justification for divine right, this particular interchange is emblematic of Locke's approach. Whether one agrees with Locke's conclusions or not, it is evident that Locke is approaching Scripture with a literal grammatical historical

---

[30] Locke, 16.
[31] Locke, 23.

approach in these contexts – even making extensive appeal to the Hebrew vocabulary and grammar of the Genesis account – while Filmer is content to employ a theological hermeneutic allowing him to make self-justified suppositions. It is no coincidence then that Locke's conclusion would be such a stark contrast to Filmer's. For Locke, all humanity are equal; for Filmer, there is integral inequity, and slavery belongs to all at one point or another.

Once he had destroyed Filmer's divine right "fatherhood" explanation of governmental authority, Locke would argue at length in his *Second Treatise* that the basis of government was rooted in natural law as given by the Creator. This natural law has embedded within it the idea of universal equality and liberty and universal responsibility: "The state of Nature has a law of Nature to govern it, which obliges every one, and reason, which is that law, teaches all mankind who will but consult it, that being all equal and independent, no one ought to harm another in his life, health, liberty or possessions; for men being all the workmanship of one omnipotent and infinitely wise Maker; all the servants of one sovereign Master, sent into the world by His order and about His business; they are His property, whose workmanship they are made to last during His, not one another's pleasure."[32]

Locke identifies here such an important principle, that all humanity belong to God and for His own pleasure. It is because of this stewardship of life that life, liberty, and the pursuit of happiness have their true value. It is this foundational concept that guides Locke's perception of the grounding of authority, as this state of nature demands that all humanity collectively have

---

[32] Locke, 107.

"the right to punish the transgressors of that law to such a degree as may hinder its violation."[33] Locke's concept of government agrees with Genesis 9:6, which provides the first direct legislation of human enforcement against unlawful activity (specifically, the violating of the image of God through the act of murder), and is consistent with Romans 13:3-4 which warns the reader that there is no need to fear authority if one does good, for authority (a punisher and wrathbringer against those who do evil) bears the sword as a servant of God .

Locke acknowledges the universal and natural freedom of all humanity, and that freedom cannot be infringed, because "This freedom from absolute, arbitrary power is so necessary to, and closely joined with, a man's preservation, that he cannot part with it but by what forfeits his preservation and life together."[34] Freedom under government is then that freedom to abide by a societal standard – standards agreed upon by those participating. Locke is hinting at a government of the people, by the people, and for the people. Slavery was another matter, and a totally unacceptable one. For Locke this meant that people must use their ability to reason as an expression of their freedom and to protect that freedom: "The freedom then of man, and liberty of acting according to his own will, is grounded on his having reason, which is able to instruct him in that law he is to govern himself by, and make him know how far he is left to the freedom of his own will. To turn him loose to an unrestrained liberty, before he has reason to guide him, is not the allowing him the privilege of his nature to be free, but to thrust him out amongst brutes, and abandon him to a state as wretched and as

---

[33] Locke, 108.
[34] Locke, 114.

much beneath that of a man as theirs."[35] It is here that the responsibility of parental education is apparent. Whereas Filmer argued for parental rule as the foundation of government, Locke argues that parental authority is designed for education unto the appropriate use and preservation of individual liberty.

MARX'S AND ENGELS' ECONOMIC SOLUTION

Karl Marx (1818-1883) and Friedrich Engels (1820-1895) proposed that the human problem was borne of class struggle and the resulting oppression of one class by another.[36] That oppression was expressed through four epochs of world history, all representing the struggle between oppressor and oppressed: (1) primitive and communal, (2) slave, (3) feudal, and (4) capitalist. Marx and Engels argued that a fifth era – a socialist and communist epoch – would resolve the issue once and for all, bringing in a golden age of equality and justice. This solution was rooted in the view of all history as economic history, thus the problem was an economic problem, and the solution was likewise an economic one. That solution was "summed up in the single sentence: abolition of private property."[37]

Marx and Engels suggested that private property had already been abolished for most, as "private property is already done away with for nine-tenths of the population; its existence for the few is solely due to its non-existence in the hands of those

---

[35] Locke, 131.
[36] Karl Marx and Friedrich Engels, *The Communist Manifesto* (New York: Penguin Books, 1967),95.
[37] Marx and Engels, 96.

nine-tenths."[38] The implications of the elimination of private property (as a tool of oppression) were broad, and necessitated the "abolition of the family,"[39] and the use of familial relations as engines of commerce. In order to rescue children from the evils of oppression, education would be made public and removed from the ruling class and their privatized education.[40]

The summary focus of this economic solution – socialism and communism – "abolishes eternal truths, it abolishes all religion and all morality, instead of constituting them on a new basis."[41] These ends "can be attained only by the forcible overthrow of all existing social conditions."[42] Because the problem is diagnosed simply as economic, there is no focus on the tethering of justice to anything other than an economic system – no justification of *why justice matters.* There is only an appeal to those dissatisfied by their current conditions to overthrow the economic powers of the day in order to seek their own betterment. Marx and Engels advocate a system that was in their time a modern expression of Plato's ideal city state governance – rule by the enlightened few to ensure that the common people are protected from themselves. "Communism sets out to free the human condition from the greed that so entangles us and that ultimately facilitates our own enslavement. Communism is most ambitious in its diagnosis of the human condition (greed, oppression) and in its prescription for redeeming the human condition (the abolition of all private property, and the dissolution of every societal force promulgated

---

[38] Marx and Engels, 98.
[39] Marx and Engels, 99.
[40] Marx and Engels, 100.
[41] Marx and Engels, 103.
[42] Marx and Engels, 120.

by the existence of capital). In communism, morality (albeit entirely redefined) is legislated to the utmost."[43]

Because the communist ideal views the proper state of nature as the appropriate economic conditions to ensure the absence of oppression, individual liberties are not advocated. It is the very expression of those liberties that is perceived as creating the oppressive conditions. Rather than allowing people to independently and from parents learn to reason and express their freedoms and responsibilities well, the socialist communist agenda co-opts parentage and education in order to ensure that none pursue individualistic interests. Private property – that very thing that Locke considered as a means of personal preservation and the preservation of liberties – cannot have a place if the collective is put before the individual. Of course the *Manifesto* makes no appeal to Scripture for its claims, for if it did, it would have to contend with the likes of Locke who would challenge the reliability of the exegesis and encourage the reader to use their own reason to assess and critique the system – choosing for themselves whether to participate or not.

ADAM SMITH'S PROPERTY AS EXPRESSION OF FREEDOM

Building on Locke's foundation, Adam Smith (1723-1790) viewed property and wealth as a necessary expression of individual liberty, not only for subsistence but for the well-ordered life: "Neither is wealth necessary merely because it affords the means of subsistence: without it we should never be able to cultivate and improve the higher and nobler faculties.

---

[43] Christopher Cone, "The Inherent Limitation of Government" in *Biblical Worldview Applied* (Fort Worth, TX: Exegetica Publishing, 2016), 195.

Where wealth has not been amassed, every one being constantly in providing for his immediate wants has no time left for the culture of the mind; and the views, sentiments, and feelings of the people become alike contracted, selfish, and illiberal...The acquisition of wealth is, in fact, quite indispensable to the advancement of society in civilization and refinement."[44] Smith recognizes that society is able to flourish when the appropriate handling of wealth is in place. He suggests that, "The number and eminence of our philosophers, poets, scholars, and artists have always increased proportionally to increase of the public wealth, or to the means of rewarding and honoring their labors."[45] Smith even acknowledges that the concept of free trade allows the sharing of wealth, and that God spread out the resources of the planet so that there would be global and free trade among all: "For the God of heaven and earth, greatly providing for mankinde, would not that all things should be found in one region, to the ende that one should have need of another; that, by this means, friendship might be established among all men, and every one seek to gratifie all."[46] Because of this principle, Smith advocates for only minimal regulation of commerce. He postulates that "Had government been able to act according to its sense of what was most for the public advantage, without being influenced by the narrow views and prejudices of the manufacturing and commercial classes, there seem to be

---

[44] Adam Smith, *An Inquiry Into the Nature and Causes of the Wealth of Nations* (Edinburgh: Adam and Chalres Black and William Tait, 1837), xv-xvi.
[45] Adam Smith, xvi.
[46] From a 1553 letter to Sir Hugh Willoughby and Richard Chancellor, in Adam Smith, xxv.

good grounds for thinking that there would have been, comparatively, few restrictions on industry."[47]

While Locke focused on the basic premises of government, Adam Smith delineates the expressions of appropriate government in economic contexts, specifically related to property and wealth. Smith's conclusions are directly contrary to those of Marx and Engels, as Marx and Engels are working from a Platonic platform of the elite making choices for the populace, while Locke and Smith are working from an altogether different platform that *the individual* rather than the collective is most important, because individuals are imbued by God with His image, and consequently, possess certain rights.

THE DECLARATION OF INDEPENDENCE: THE NECESSITY AND PRIORITY OF RIGHTS

The Declaration of Independence attributes the rights of individuals and government to "the Laws of Nature and of Nature's God."[48] By virtue of all humanity being created equal,[49] all equally are "endowed by their Creator with certain unalienable rights."[50] These rights are integral to human existence, and their description as unalienable means they *cannot* be removed from the individual. The Declaration orders the rights by logical priority: "Life, Liberty, and the Pursuit of Happiness."[51] Without life, one cannot have liberty, and without

---

[47] Adam Smith, xxv.
[48] The Declaration of Independence: A Transcription, viewed at https://www.archives.gov/founding-docs/declaration-transcript.
[49] Declaration of Independence.
[50] Declaration of Independence.
[51] Declaration of Independence.

liberty one cannot pursue happiness. The order of these rights is no coincidence, and it is by failing to recognize the order of importance in priority that they are often violated. For example, the pro-choice platform argues that "the government should not intrude into an area of intimate, private decision-making...Instead, the government should remain neutral on the issue of childbearing and allow people to make their own decisions."[52] This thinking emphasizes the woman's personal liberty, which is at first glance a wonderful thing. However, the grave error is that it prioritizes the woman's personal liberty over the unborn's right to life. The current Democratic Platform includes this right to choose as an inherent need for the flourishing of women: "We believe that comprehensive health services, including access to reproductive care and abortion services, are vital to the empowerment of women and girls."[53] On the other side of the aisle, the Republican Platform affirms that, "The Constitution's guarantee that no one can "be deprived of life, liberty or property" deliberately echoes the Declaration of Independence's proclamation that "all" are "endowed by their Creator" with the inalienable right to life. Accordingly, we assert the sanctity of human life and affirm that the unborn child has a fundamental right to life which cannot be infringed. We support a human life amendment to the Constitution and legislation to make clear that the Fourteenth Amendment's protections apply to children before birth."[54]

---

[52] ACLU, "The Right to Choose at 25: Looking Back and Ahead" viewed at https://www.aclu.org/other/right-choose-25-looking-back-and-ahead/.
[53] The 2020 Democratic Party Platform, 82, viewed at https://www.demconvention.com/wp-content/uploads/2020/08/2020-07-31-Democratic-Party-Platform-For-Distribution.pdf.
[54] The 2020 Republican Party Platform, 13, viewed at https://prod-cdn-static.gop.com/docs/Resolution_Platform_2020.pdf.

The order of these rights matters immensely, and violating the order of these rights violates the Declaration and the Constitution which guarantees and protects the three unalienable rights. Consequently, any violation of these three rights represents tyranny, and reasonable justification for peoples to "dissolve the political bands which have connected them with another."[55] By implication no governing authority has the right to violate these rights and any authority that does so represents political bands which may rightly dissolved. In acknowledging these bands, the Declaration is asserting that no person has the right to rule over another in a way that violates these rights. Based on self-evident natural law created by God, the three essential human rights are the necessary condition for governmental authority. Natural law supersedes governmental law, as governmental law is (or ought to be) an outworking of natural law.

Because God as Creator supersedes natural law, lack of submission to governmental powers that usurp these inherent human rights imbued by God is no violation of legitimate authority, and thus the Declaration can call upon people to "throw off such Government, and to provide new guards for their future security."[56] This is revolution without rebellion. The Declaration advocates governmental overthrow, and its authors knew full well Paul's mandate that "every person is to be in subjection to the governing authorities"[57] Perhaps they also understood the passage as having an important qualification. Those who are governing (ὑπερεχούσαις) are not necessarily authoritative. Only those who are governing and actually *are*

---

[55] Declaration of Independence.
[56] Declaration of Independence.
[57] Romans 13:1a.

authorities (ἐξουσίαις) are subject to this kind of submission. Paul says nothing of tyrannical rulers or those who are usurping authority, but rather he addresses those who actually are authorities as having authority established by God Himself.[58] Therefore, the one resisting the authority (τῇ ἐξουσίᾳ) is resisting God Himself.[59] Nonetheless, we cannot read Romans through the lens of the Declaration, instead we must view the Declaration through the lens of Romans.

BIBLICAL ASSERTIONS OF INDIVIDUAL CIVIL LIBERTIES

It is evident that Paul wrote his Letter to the Romans during a time of tyranny and unjust rulership. He wrote the letter in 56-57,[60] during Nero's rule – one of the most oppressive administrations in Roman history. While he generally set a submissive and respectful tone, the trajectory of his entire ministry was impacted by a continuous civil disobedience on his part. First, before he became a believer in and follower of Christ, he was an enforcer against those who were violating the law in following Christ.[61] After his conversion, Paul was proclaiming the gospel of that very Christ, was imprisoned for doing so, and kept proclaiming the good news of Jesus anyway.[62] He encountered state and civil sanctions on numerous occasions,[63] yet remained undeterred. Like Peter who said, "We must obey

---

[58] Romans 13:1b.
[59] Romans 13:2.
[60] Christopher Cone, *A Concise Bible Survey: Tracing the Promises of God,* 4th Edition (Fort Worth, TX: Exegetica Publishing, 2012), 216.
[61] Acts 8-9.
[62] E.g., Acts 16.
[63] 2 Corinthians 11:23-26.

God rather than men,"[64] Paul's own actions help provide context and qualification of his exhortation that believers be submissive to governing authorities. Paul understood both the Source and the nature of true authority, and he recognized that those two concepts were intertwined with the idea of individual liberties – both by nature, and in Christ.

Humanity was created uniquely in the image of God, and as such enjoyed a different relationship to nature than the rest of creation.[65] Animals were not described as being morally accountable for how they treated each other, but they were held morally accountable for their treatment of human life.[66] Further, humanity was mandated to enforce the sanctity of the *imago dei* in humanity.[67] It is in this context that we find the first mandate for human government, and it is directly connected with the sanctity of life *for every individual human.*

Within the Mosaic Law not only was God concerned with national interests, but He also paid close attention to individual interests. The last six of the Ten Commandments dealt with actions toward individuals.[68] In fact, God was so considerate of individual liberties – after establishing the individual's right to life – that He even protected their "right" to possess, without molestation, their own personal property.[69]

While God is sovereign over governments,[70] He also works through the vessels of human governments, appointing

---

[64] Acts 5:29.

[65] Genesis 1:26-28.

[66] Genesis 9:5.

[67] Genesis 9:6.

[68] Exodus 20:12-17.

[69] E.g., Exodus 20:17b – "or anything that belongs to your neighbor."

[70] Job 12:23, Psalm 22:28, 47:8, 75:7,82:8, Isaiah 40:15-17,

kings and holding them accountable.[71] When Jesus instructed His listeners to render to Caesar what was Caesar's, He wasn't taking a *laissez faire* approach to human government, rather He was illustrating how people could recognize the limitation of human government, not of His own. As had been prophesied long prior, there would be no end to His government.[72] In that future kingdom economy there is individual responsibility and individual blessing – happiness.[73]

In the present age individual liberties are expressed in the phrase "Love does no wrong to a neighbor."[74] Love cannot infringe on one's Biblical right to life,[75] nor on one's personal liberty (or freedoms) except their own freedoms on behalf of another,[76] nor on one's pursuit of happiness – if happiness is defined as blessing, which comes from right relationship with the Lord and proper application of that position in relationship with others.[77] Even in the body of Christ which is one, there are many members. Each plays a vital role,[78] and each has a manifestation of the Holy Spirit for the common good.[79] As Peter later explains, each believer is gifted for the purpose of glorifying Him through serving one another.[80] There is an incredible balance between personal liberties and personal responsibilities. Without the one, the other cannot be met.

---

[71] E.g., 1 Samuel 13, Daniel 4, etc.
[72] E.g., Daniel 2:44-45.
[73] Jeremiah 31:29-30, 34-35.
[74] Romans 13:10.
[75] Genesis 9:6.
[76] 1 Corinthians 11:23-24, 31-33.
[77] E.g., Matthew 18:6, 19:14.
[78] 1 Corinthians 12:12-27.
[79] 1 Corinthians 12:7.
[80] 1 Peter 4:10-11.

In taking these passages at face value, we recognize that God first provides a platform wherein we can understand what He has said and what He intends (epistemology). Then, He has revealed to us the realities of which He wants us to be aware (metaphysics). Once we understand the realities and have confidence that we have understood Him, we can understand what we should do about all this (ethics), and how we should interact with each other (socio-political thought). For Plato, Filmer, Marx, Engels, and other thinkers who are not beginning with God as authoritative (Filmer begins with God, but enthrones himself as interpreter of Scripture), their understanding of the nature of the individual and their rights and liberties is distorted. On the other hand, with the literal grammatical historical understanding of Scripture, we end up with similar conclusions as Locke, Smith, and the writers of the Declaration – these who recognize that all humanity possesses unalienable rights to life, liberty, and the pursuit of fulfillment and blessing by knowing God and utilizing that which He has given to us.

CHAPTER 2

HOW DID WE GET HERE?
COMPETING THEORIES OF ORIGIN

"How did we get here?" This is one of the great questions of life, and its answer sets the direction for so many other answers to great questions. If we are descended from animals, then are we not justified in living as animals? If we are generated merely by chance, then is there any meaning to life, or do we simply make our own? If we are created by a non-involved creator, then are we accountable to that creator? If we are created by the Creator described in the Bible, then are we not accountable to Him, and should we not look to Him to guide in our understanding of existence in His universe?

How we answer the origin question in large part predetermines how we view and answer questions of our own personal meaning and responsibility. We really can't know what we should do unless we know who we are. And we can't know who we are unless we know from whence we came.

There are two major categories of origin theories: abiogenesis (that life comes from nonlife) and biogenesis (that life comes from life). Abiogenesis tries to explain existence and what we observe based on the presupposition that there is nothing beyond the isolated system of the natural realm.

Abiogenesis presupposes an internally driven, self-created, and self-contained system. Biogenesis, on the other hand, presupposes something or someone outside the natural realm that exerted itself in the formation or creation of the natural realm and life in it. Biogenesis presupposes an externally driven system created by something or someone outside of the system, with minimal interaction (in a closed system biogenesis theory) or with broad interaction (in an open system biogenesis theory).

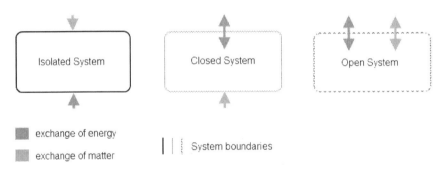

Figure 1[81]

Using thermodynamic systems to illustrate, an isolated system does not allow anything in or out; a closed system allows heat but not matter in and out; and an open system allows both in and out. Abiogenesis theories presuppose the universe as an isolated system with nothing interacting from the outside. A closed system biogenesis theory would allow for some degree of

---

[81] Bio-Physics Wiki, "Isolated Closed and Open Systems" viewed at http://www.bio-physics.at/wiki/index.php?title=Isolated_Closed_and_Open_Systems.

interaction (in deism, for example, God creates, but is not otherwise accessible to His creation) with an external force. An open system biogenesis acknowledges interaction between the universe and that which is outside it.

In the isolated system, meaning is found only from within. In the closed system, there is some connection to the outside, with minimal practical implication. In an open system the external interacts with the internal and influences the existence of the internal far beyond simple causation. Whether or not the universe is isolated, closed, or open is significant in our understanding of our origin and purpose.

ABIOGENESIS THEORIES (ISOLATED SYSTEM)

Big Bang

In 1929 Edwin Hubble observed other galaxies moving away from our own in all directions with great speed, suggesting an incredible initial force. This is either reflective of an expanding universe or the contents of that universe moving toward the outer boundary. In either case, this phenomenon is compatible with the Big Bang theory that the universe was begun by an initial cataclysmic explosion. In 1931 Georges Lemaitre proposed his theory that the expanding universe had begun from an initial primeval atom or cosmic egg.[82]

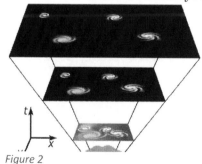

Figure 2

---

[82] The Physics of the Universe, "Georges Lemaitre" in Important Scientists, viewed at

Panspermia

In the panspermia theory, the universe has within it the ingredients of life, and over the course of a great deal of time, and through motion and internal transference, those ingredients eventually mixed to form life. The recent discovery of survival in space of a tiny eight-legged animal provides evidence that the transportation of living things through space is a viable concept.[83]

There are several related views that the ingredients of life were already on earth and were combined as ice melted, as lightning struck, as clay mixed, through volcanic activity, through submarine hydrothermal vents, through RNA residing in the primordial soup, or even through aliens planting life on earth.

Thermodynamic Dissipation Theory of the Origin of Life

Physicist Karo Michaelian postulated a model in which ribonucleic acid (RNA) and deoxyribonucleic acid (DNA) are "reproduced without the need for enzymes, promoted instead through UV light dissipation and diurnal temperature cycling of the Archean sea-surface."[84] Michaelian sees this view as advantageous over other prevailing theories in that it "does not require *the unlikely discovery of an abiotic mechanism* that

---

http://www.physicsoftheuniverse.com/scientists_lemaitre.html. And see Figure 2, from The Physics of the Universe, "The Expanding Universe and Hubble's Law" in The Big Bang and the Big Crunch, viewed at http://www.physicsoftheuniverse.com/topics_bigbang_expanding.html.
[83] http://www.space.com/5843-legged-space-survivor-panspermia-life.html?_ga=2.117209410.515311550.1494592683-1703505963.1494590890.
[84] K. Michaelian, "Thermodynamic Dissipation Theory of the Origin of Life" in *Earth System Dynamics*, March 11, 2011: 37.

produced an initial high enrichment of chiral enantiomers to explain the homochirality of life today [emphasis mine]."[85] Rather than relying on a random accident to provide the impetus for life, Michaelian suggests that the ingredients (RNA and DNA, specifically) are purposefully reproduced through UV light dissipation for specific effect: "the net effect of the origin and evolution of life has been to gradually increase the Earth's entropy producing potential."[86] The origin and evolution of life was and is goal oriented, universal, and involves a strong coupling of biotic and abiotic processes moving toward disorder.[87]

What is perhaps most interesting about each of these origin theories of life is that they are not actually origin theories. They all presuppose the eternal existence of matter, energy, and motion. While they try to explain how life comes into existence from non-life, they make no effort to address where those initial ingredients originated, other than to say, as did Carl Sagan, "The Cosmos is all that is ever was or ever will be."[88]

BIOGENESIS THEORIES (CLOSED SYSTEM)

Deism

Former atheist Antony Flew, in his autobiographical and philosophical treatise *There is a God*, traces his personal journey and explains how he arrived at a belief in the existence of God. He holds to a tentative style of deism, believing that God resembles Aristotle's version, not engaging in the affairs of the

---

[85] Ibid.: 47.
[86] Ibid.: 48.
[87] Ibid.
[88] Carl Sagan, *Cosmos* (New York, Ballantine, 1985), 1.

world.[89] Flew argues that the universe was created, but sees no direct current involvement of such a Creator, though he admits an openness to learning more about that Creator.[90]

In chapters 6-10 of *Book XII* of his *Metaphysics*, Aristotle argues for a single prime mover – an eternal unmovable substance – who must be imperishable. Aristotle doesn't speak of this deity as personal in the sense of being engaged in the natural world, but rather primarily as causative. As Aristotle held that God was a metaphysical perfection, Aristotle's God could not contemplate anything less than Himself, and thus could not engage in nature lets He fall out of metaphysical perfection.[91] Aristotle's perspective of God is a deistic one.

Intelligent Design

Philosopher of Science Stephen Meyer suggests that information is a fundamental ingredient of life, and that it can be traced back to intelligence in design. Intelligent Design (ID) is akin to deism, but is less reliant on a personal deity – though some proponents of ID are theists. Meyer is careful to distinguish ID from creationism, noting its origins in the 60's and 70's as a scientific movement arising from recognitions of fine tuning in the laws of physics.[92] Meyer suggests that "the information-bearing properties of DNA, the miniature circuits and machines in cells and the fine tuning of the laws and

---

[89] Antony Flew, *There is a God* (New York, HarperOne, 2008), 156.

[90] Ibid., 156-157.

[91] Stanley Sfekas, "Aristotle's Concept of God" in *An Esoteric Quest for The Mysteries and Philosophies of Antiquity*, Sept. 3-8, 2008, viewed at http://www.academia.edu/15234171/ARISTOTLES_CONCEPT_OF_GOD.

[92] Stephen Meyer, "A Scientific and Philosophical Defense of the Theory of Intelligent Design" Discovery Institute, Oct. 7, 2008, viewed at http://www.discovery.org/a/7471.

constants of physics...are best explained by an intelligent cause rather than an undirected material process."[93] Meyer is also careful to note that ID is not counter to Darwinian evolution, but only contradicts "Darwin's idea that the cause of biological change is wholly blind and undirected."[94]

BIOGENESIS THEORIES (OPEN SYSTEM)

Theistic Evolution / BioLogos

Geneticist Francis Collins, argues for a contemporary version of theistic evolution in his *The Language of God: A Scientist Presents Evidence for Belief*. He warns that a *God-in-the-gaps* approach is doomed as science makes progress, and he views evolutionary theory as fundamental progress, suggesting that "Darwin's framework of variation and natural selection...is unquestionably correct."[95] He adds that his "BioLogos" concept "will not go out of style or be disproven by future scientific discoveries. It is intellectually rigorous and provides answers to many otherwise puzzling questions."[96]

Gap Theory

The publishing of Charles Lyell's *Principles of Geology,* beginning in 1830, proposed uniformitarianism and an old earth view as science through the interpretation of geological ages. In order to accommodate Lyell's science, C.I. Scofield's Study Bible and Clarence Larkin's *Dispensational Truth* helped popularize

---

[93] Ibid.
[94] Ibid.
[95] Francis Collins, T*he Language of God: A Scientist Presents Evidence for Belief* (New York, NY: Free Press, 2006), 141.
[96] Ibid., 210.

the view that there was a gap of indeterminate time between Genesis 1:1 and 1:2. This gap accomplished two things: (1) it allowed time within a Biblical framework for Lyell's geological ages, and (2) it provided a convenient time window for the fall of Satan (and in some iterations of the gap theory, a great war between God and Satan). Proponents of the gap theory view the theory as *compatible* with an exegetical approach, even though it requires reading between the lines of the first two verse in Genesis. Scofield, for example suggests that Jeremiah 4:23-26 is referring to the Genesis 1:2 world and, "describes the condition of the earth as the result of judgment...which overthrew the primal order of Gen 1:1."[97]

Progressive Creationism

Astrophysicist Hugh Ross views the heavens as having been stretched out and continuing to be stretched out, and he connects this process with Lemaitre's big bang:

> This simultaneously finished and ongoing aspect of cosmic stretching is identical to the big bang concept of cosmic expansion. According to the big bang, at the creation event all the physics (specifically, the laws, constants, and equations of physics) are instantly created, designed, and finished so as to guarantee an ongoing, continual expansion of the universe at exactly the right rates with respect to time so that physical life will be possible.[98]

---

[97] C.I. Scofield, Scofield Reference Bible, 1917, 776.
[98] http://www.reasons.org/articles/big-bang---the-bible-taught-it-first.

Ross' view is that God used the big bang to create life:

> From 4.5 to 3.8 billion years ago, an unusually large number of comets and asteroids bombarded Earth's surface – particularly toward the end of this period. Many of these collisions would have liquefied the crust hundreds of meters deep, nearly (if not completely) sterilizing the planet. The scientific data shows an abundance of life right after the intense bombardment ceased – in the absence of any evidence for a prebiotic or primordial soup. Multiple lines of evidences also indicate a high level of complexity for this first life. While evolutionary models strain to accommodate this scientific data – and also struggle to explain how life can originate from non-life (called abiogenesis) – the evidence affirms [Reason to Believe's] creation model.[99]

Ross's (and Reason to Believe's) view is old earth with a day age view of the creation week,[100] and that we are currently in the seventh day or an age of God resting from creation.[101] Holding to this day age model, Ross and RTB deny evolution as ungrounded, unnecessary, and incompatible with Scripture.

Young Earth Creationism

In addition to being a commonly held understanding throughout church history, young earth creationism represents the most literal reading of the Genesis creation account and

---

[99] Ibid.
[100] http://www.reasons.org/rtb-101/biblicalevidenceforanoldearth.
[101] Ibid.

accompanying passages.[102] Young earth creationism views Genesis 1:1 and 1:2 not as separated by a gap, but as narrative of a single event beginning the first day of creation week. Each of the six creation days (including the three preceding the creation of the sun) begin with evening and end with morning. The creation week culminates with the seventh day rest, which God set apart from the other days to denote His completed work (Gen 2:3-4). Young earth creationism pursues and acknowledges scientific data but challenges interpretive presuppositions of other theories which presuppose an old earth (i.e., through uniformitarian assumptions).

THE EPISTEMOLOGICAL PIVOT

Upon what epistemological basis do each of these theories ground themselves? How would we come to prefer one over the others? Each of the theories process observable phenomena in light of the presuppositions which ground the theories. To assess the value of the theories we have to distill them down to the presuppositions upon which they are built. Abiogenesis isolated system theories, rooted in empiricism, presuppose the absence of the supernatural since it cannot be observed with empirical tools (the senses). If those tools are accurate and capable of measuring *all* of reality, then theories emerging from empiricism are plausible. Biogenesis closed systems theories synthesize empiricism and rationalism in order to account for a higher, creative power that seems not to be exclusively within the universe. This approach relies on empiricism, but views it as

---

[102] Christopher Cone, "The History of Biblical/Scientific Creationism in the Church" in *The Genesis Factor*, ed. Ron J Bigalke Jr., (Greek Forest, AR: Master Books, 2008), 21-42.

somewhat limited and appeals to a rationalistic tendency of recognize the dependence of the internal on the external.

Biogenesis open system theories rely primarily on special revelation as the fundamental principle, but to differing degrees these theories appeal to empiricism as a lens through which to view special revelation. For example, Hugh Ross' progressive creationism, the gap theory, and theistic evolution all view the Scriptures as authoritative but interpret them through an empirical lens. In contrast to these models, young earth creationism relies on Scripture as understood through the literal grammatical historical hermeneutic. This latter view welcomes empirical data but recognizes the limits of empirical as not exceeding the boundaries of Scripture. Consequently, in choosing to prefer one theory of origin over another, the interlocutor is not merely choosing a narrative, he or she is choosing an entire worldview. The question is which epistemological grounding is the correct one. The right answer to that question helps us arrive with confidence at who we are, from whence we came, and what we should do.

CHAPTER 3
BIBLICAL SOCIO-POLITICAL FOUNDATIONS

Dispensationalists have been accused of, among other things,[103] being pessimistic (as by Marsden and Bube)[104] and

---

[103] Tweeted by @Ligioner, 1/20/2012, 8:26pm: "Why aren't you a dispensationalist?" R.C. Sproul replied, "Because I think that dispensational theology is goofy." http://www.ligonier.org/blog/twitter-highlights-12212/; "Dispensational pre-millennialism typically causes a predisposition toward pessimism in world affairs and a general worsening of international relations. A pre-millennial reading of Bible prophecy paints a dismal picture of a world disintegrating toward a cataclysmic end where we are forced to confront the wrath and judgment of God. Assumptions and plans based on this worldview will be less than ideal" (Major Brian L. Stuckert, "Strategic Implications of American Millennialism," Monograph submitted to School of Advanced Military Studies United States Army Command and General Staff College Fort Leavenworth, Kansas, 2008.).

[104] "This view [premillennialism] emphasizes the pessimism of the present day, in which we can look forward to nothing more than continued degradation of the world and disintegration of human society until Christ returns to establish justice and righteousness by His power" (Richard H. Bube, "Optimism and Pessimism: Science and Eschatology, in *JETS*, Fall 1972; 217.); "The area where dispensationalists were perhaps most out of step with the rest of nineteenth-century thinking was in their view of contemporary history, which had little or no room for social or political progress. When they spoke on this question, dispensational premillennialists were characteristically pessimistic" (George Marsden, *Fundamentalism and American Culture: The Shaping*

anti-Semitic (as by Wilson),[105] in large part due to the premillennial understanding of Biblical eschatology. However, upon exegetical consideration of several foundational prerequisites of Biblical socio-political thought, it is evident that Biblical socio-political undergirding in fact *requires* the premillennial understanding, and that such an understanding affords dispensational thinkers an appropriate (i.e., Biblical) degree of care, realism, and constructiveness for the world around us. In short, owing much to the premillennial understanding, dispensational thinking – far from being a hindrance to the progress of society – is a great benefit to society. This has profound and far-reaching practical implications not only for dispensational thought, but also for practical ministry in the church and for interaction with those outside the church.

Prolegomena

A Biblical worldview, by definition, must include at least two characteristics: (1) it must be Biblical – derived exclusively from the Biblical record, and (2) it must be, in fact, a worldview – that is to say it should be, as Vidal puts it, a "collection of concepts allowing us to 'construct a global image of the world, and in this way to understand as many elements of our

---

of Twentieth Century Evangelicalism 1870-1925 (Oxford: Oxford University Press, 1980), 66.).

[105] "It is regrettable that this view [that Gentiles are occasionally instruments of God's retribution on Israel] allowed premillennialists to expect the phenomenon of anti-Semitism and tolerate it matter-of-factly" (Dwight Wilson, *Armageddon Now! The Premillenarian Response to Russia and Israel Since 1917* (Tyler, TX: Institute for Christian Economics, 1991), 16.).

experience as possible.'"[106] Vidal's characterization of worldview is consistent with the German concept of *Weltanshauung*[107] as foundational, internally cohesive, and comprehensive – three important traits for a *meaningful* worldview.

Foundational

A Biblical worldview should be foundational, in that it works from the ground up. This is a challenge for historical dispensationalism, which has been largely considered an extraction from Reformed theology with but a few reformations of its own. Rather than viewing dispensational thought as a Biblical outworking that stands independently and as constructed purely on Biblical foundations, we sometimes perceive dispensationalism as a refocusing of Reformed theology especially in the areas of eschatology and ecclesiology.[108] But as we begin to acknowledge that dispensationalism is not a hermeneutic through which we view the Bible, but is instead the result of the Bible examined through a particular method (the literal grammatical historical hermeneutic), we may recognize the necessity of attending to the foundational aspects of dispensational thought instead of simply borrowing foundations from other theological traditions.

---

[106] C. Vidal, (2008) Wat is een wereldbeeld? (What is a worldview?), in Van Belle, H. & Van der Veken, J., Editors, *Nieuwheid denken. De wetenschappen en het creatieve aspect van de werkelijkheid,* in press. Acco, Leuven; 3.

[107] German: worldview.

[108] Perhaps this is one reason dispensationalism has lacked historically in the development of worldview in favor of works on ecclesiology and eschatology.

Internally Cohesive

A Biblical worldview must also be internally cohesive, in that its components should fit together and should progress in some logical sequence. Much like Paul describes the church as built on the cornerstone that is Christ and on the foundation of the apostles and prophets, and as being built up with all the saints, there is a logical flow and interconnectedness in a meaningful worldview. That progress demands an internal consistency in the sense that one area of examination cannot contradict another without the whole being undermined. If one logically necessary subset fails, then the category that birthed the subset is flawed and untenable with respect to truth. Because a Biblical worldview purports to be grounded in *truth*, any single inconsistency within the system breaks down the whole system as untrustworthy. Hence, consistency is paramount in the development of this or any other system.

Comprehensive

In light of the global implications of *Weltanshauung*, a Biblical worldview must be comprehensive in that if it is derived from a source that claims to be sufficient for the adequacy and equipping of its believers for every good work (2 Tim 3:16-17), it must, in fact, be sufficient to that end, lest it violate (1) the principle of internal cohesiveness or consistency and (2) its own foundational truth claim. Consequently, the jurisdiction of a Biblical worldview is unlimited, and there is no field of inquiry on which the Bible cannot shed at least some foundational light. It is in this sense that Ryrie suggests that the Scriptures provide a comprehensive philosophy of history. His comments to this effect are worth consideration here:

The Scriptures per se are not a philosophy of history, but they contain one. It is true that the Bible deals with ideas- but with ideas that are interpretations of historical events. This interpretation of the meaning of historical events is the task of theology, and it is a task that is not without its problems. The chief problem is that both covenant and dispensational theologies claim to represent the true philosophy of history as contained in the Scriptures. The problem is further complicated by the fact that, if a philosophy of history is defined as "a systematic interpretation of universal history in accordance with a principle by which historical events and successions are unified and directed toward ultimate meaning," then in a certain sense both systems of theology meet the basic requirements of the definition. However, the way in which the two systems meet these requirements affirms that dispensationalism is the more valid and helpful system. Notice that the definition centers on three things: (1) the recognition of "historical events and successions," or a proper concept of the progress of revelation in history; (2) the unifying principle; and (3) the ultimate goal of history. Let us examine both systems in relation to these three features.[109]

Notice Ryrie's (correct) perception that theology needs to be more broadly explanatory than simply offering commentary on a few religious issues, that it is closely related to philosophy, and

---

[109] Charles C. Ryrie, *Dispensationalism*, Revised and Expanded (Chicago, IL: Moody Press, 1995), 16.

that of the two major models (dispensationalism and Covenant theology) which attempt to account for human experience, dispensationalism offers the best philosophy of history. Ryrie's thoughts here underscore the importance of a foundational, internally cohesive, and fully comprehensive model, and he asserts that dispensationalism is the best model in those regards.

Components and Grounding of a Biblical Worldview

Recognizing seven particular components is helpful for addressing the necessity for a worldview to be both foundational and comprehensive. In logical order of consideration from the perspective of the inquirer,[110] we undertake these seven steps as they build successively on each other – each being grounded on the conclusions of the previous step. (1) Epistemology, as the study of knowledge and the first step in the worldview inquiry, helps us arrive at understanding how we can know with certainty the answers to all the other steps. In short, epistemology considers the source of authority for all other inquiry. (2) Ontology builds on that foundation by appealing to the source of authority confirmed in the epistemological inquiry and explains what is the reality around us. Ontology is the inquiry about what actually exists. (3) Teleology explains why that which exists does indeed exist. Teleology considers purpose and relies wholly on the epistemological conclusions for its basis.

---

[110] Or course, the perspective of the inquirer isn't always the best perspective. In this discussion we consider epistemology before metaphysical issues, because the epistemological question must be addressed first by the inquirer in order to understand the metaphysical question. However, the metaphysical reality exists with or without the inquirer's understanding, and thus comes first in reality. This issue is addressed in *Appendix I*.

(4) Eschatology is only possible insofar as the epistemological source of authority reveals what the future will hold and is a necessary prerequisite to worldview components pertaining to human practice, because the concepts of reward and consequence are purely eschatological. (5) Axiology answers questions regarding value and the nature of good and evil, and is closely akin to teleology, as purpose determines function and makes obvious what is good and what is not. (6) Praxeology moves the inquirer from *is* to *ought* – from descriptive to prescriptive – and serves as the *therefore* in the worldview series of inquiry. The term praxeology, as employed here, refers to the behavior and ethics required of individuals by the axiological conclusions. (7) Sociopraxy extrapolates praxeological conclusions to the societal level: whereas praxeology considers ethics on an individual level, sociopraxy considers ethical obligations on a societal level.

These seven components fit within four major categories of philosophical pursuit: epistemology, metaphysics (includes ontology, teleology, eschatology, and axiology), ethics (praxeology), and socio-political thought (sociopraxy). It is worth noting how much of our inquiry is in the realm of metaphysics, and that in order to answer questions pertaining to metaphysics, we must have tools that are capable of addressing the metaphysics questions. Thus, epistemology is the foundational first field of inquiry.

Epistemology

Before we can take the first step in constructing (or understanding) a meaningful worldview we must discern the basis for recognizing what is true and what is not true. Without such a basis, any further pursuit is devoid of meaning, and we are left with no means to answer questions. All meaningful answers, then, are necessarily rooted in the concept of authority, and the questions themselves invite us to consider what are the overarching principles that govern our human experience.

Historically there have been many attempts at deciphering those overarching principles, but a few stand out as particularly influential. Plato's dualism (as represented by his allegory of the cave and his divided-line theory from *The Republic,* Book VII) suggests that the realm of experience offers only cursory glances at truth, but that greater enlightenment through the gaining of knowledge is necessary for the discerning of more certain truth. Plato's epistemology prescribed philosophical learning and reasoning as the path to certainty. Rene Descartes' rationalism (as represented in his *Discourse on the Method of Rightly Conducting the Reason and Seeking Truth in the Sciences*) prescribes the guided (by Descartes' method) use of human reason as the means of determining truth. David Hume's empiricism (as discussed in his *Treatise on Human Nature*) relies on human experience interpreted by the senses for the discernment of truth. Hume makes no allowance for the supernatural or metaphysical, because he asserts that we possess no tools to sense these things. Thus, for Hume reality is grounded in the natural, in what we can sense. Nietzsche abandoned the cause of the discernment of truth as grounding for meaningful worldview. Instead, he pursued his existentialist course that the only thing of which we can be certain is that any true meaning is inaccessible to us and thus irrelevant.[111] Consequently, we make our own meaning by being the best version of us we can be.

---

[111] E.g., as in *Thus Spoke Zarathustra.*

The epistemological conclusions of each of these thinkers share one thing in common: *unapologetic self-reliance for the determining of truth.* Plato relies on his understanding, Descartes on his reason, Hume on his senses, and Nietzsche on his will to power. In stark contrast, the Bible prescribes a model antithetical to the self-reliance prescribed in the aforementioned epistemological models.

The first epistemological statement in the Bible is actually made by the serpent in the Garden: "For God knows that in the day you eat from it your eyes will be opened, and you will be like God, knowing good and evil."[112] Satan prescribes knowledge through contradicting God's design for knowledge. The fact that Satan chose epistemology as an early battleground underscores the strategic significance of epistemology in God's design. In this context Satan challenges Eve to consider a different starting point than God had prescribed, and if she does, Satan promises, Eve will have a better outcome – that her knowledge will be more complete, even to the point of making her godlike. While the actions Satan prescribed did result in particular knowledge,[113] it was a distortion of God's design for knowledge and resulted in tragedy and not blessing.

These events invite the reader to inquire as to God's ideal for human knowledge, and the answer is provided especially in the writings of Solomon, to whom it was granted to be exceedingly wise.[114] In the book of Proverbs Solomon identifies the first epistemological step undergirding a Biblical worldview: "The fear of the Lord is the beginning of wisdom;"[115] "The fear of

---

[112] Genesis 3:5.
[113] Genesis 3:22.
[114] 1 Kings 3:12.
[115] Proverbs 1:7.

the Lord is the beginning of wisdom, and the knowledge of the Holy One is understanding;"[116] and again, "The fear of the Lord is the instruction for wisdom."[117] The word for *fear* is the Hebrew *yirah*, and does not simply denote respect, but is the term normally used of *fear* – as in fear for one's life.[118] In context, the fear of the Lord involves the right perspective of and response to God.[119] Though Solomon uses a different word for *fear* in Proverbs 28:14, the contrast to appropriate fear is hardness of heart.[120] In short, the fear of the Lord involves the inner man's responsiveness to God.

Notice the critique of the atheist in Psalm 14:1: "The fool has said in his heart (Heb., *leb*) 'There is no God.'" The fool is unresponsive toward God, and sets his will against God, whereas the one who would possess wisdom acknowledges God and is responsive to Him. From whence comes the fear of the Lord? "For the Lord gives wisdom; from His mouth comes wisdom and understanding."[121] If the first step or first principle of Biblical epistemology is to fear the Lord, the authoritative source for the data we need to do so is identified as Scripture itself – a revelation which presupposes the existence of the Biblical God and makes no effort to defend that first and most vital principle.

---

[116] 9:10.

[117] 15:33.

[118] E.g., Gen 15:1, 32:11; Prov 3:25, etc.

[119] Discussions regarding the fear the Lord are found also in the NT in passages such as Romans 3:18; 2 Corinthians 5:11, 7:1; Ephesians 5:21; 1 Peter 2:17; and Revelation 14:7.

[120] The Hebrew *leb*, translated here as *heart*, is generally used to reference the heart, mind, will, and/or inner man.

[121] Proverbs 2:6.

As we read the Bible, we discover therein the limitations of human reasoning, and thus, the inadequacies of learning and rationalism;[122] we encounter the limited scope of human experience and of the uninformed arrogance of naturalistic empiricism;[123] and we are met with the reality that there is indeed discernable meaning and truth – noumenal reality, created and revealed by God, and relevant for everyday human life – even if God hasn't revealed its fullness.[124] *A Biblical worldview starts with a Biblical epistemology,*[125] *which identifies the Bible itself as the source of authority for all other inquiries, in contradistinction to any other proposed source of authority.*[126]

---

[122] Genesis 6:5, 1 Corinthians 2:14.

[123] Job 38:4, 34-35, 39:26-27, 41:11, 42:5-6.

[124] Ecclesiastes 3:11, John 20:31, James 3:17-18, 1 John 5:13.

[125] Much of the material from the previous four paragraphs is adapted from Christopher Cone, "Epistemological Foundations of a Biblical Theology, or Bob's Crazy Day with the Dandelions" presented to the Chafer Theological Seminary Conference, March 12, 2014, and later published online at http://www.drcone.com/2014/03/13/epistemological-foundations-for-a-biblical-theology/.

[126] One critique of this epistemological first-principle (that the Bible is the authoritative source of truth) is that it amounts to fideism or circular reasoning. But that charge rings hollow when one recognizes that all epistemological first-principle claims (whether by Plato, Descartes, Hume, Nietzsche, or anyone else) are assumed to be self-authenticating and self-evident by those who make the claims. The very first step in any worldview system is necessarily understood to be self-evident (or else it would obviously be a second step, not a first), and its legitimacy as first-principle is generally tested by how well it corresponds to truth (correspondence theory), by the resulting worldview's internal cohesiveness and coherence (coherence theory), and for some, by how well the system actually works (pragmatic theory). I suggest that the Biblical worldview holds up well under the scrutiny of any of the three traditional theories of truth, and that the Biblical epistemological first-

The Hermeneutic Requirement of a Biblical Epistemology

Interpretive method is an integral factor in applying a Biblical epistemology. If the fear of the Lord is the beginning of wisdom,[127] and if wisdom is knowable and discernible,[128] then the fear of the Lord is knowable and discernible. If knowledge and understanding come from His mouth,[129] and if knowledge and understanding are rooted in the fear of the Lord,[130] then the fear of the Lord is discovered in His word. If these two syllogisms are valid and true, then the word of God (at least insofar as it considers the fear of the Lord) is knowable and discernible.

Even a cursory examination of Scripture gives us at least two major evidences that the Bible intends its readers to employ a particular hermeneutic method in discerning the meaning of the Bible. First, the Bible is written using three distinct human languages (Hebrew, Aramaic, and Greek), each with its own distinctive grammatical structures and vocabulary. The simple fact that these languages are employed demands that the reader respect fundamental aspects of the languages and follow literal grammatical historical principles. In order to have knowable and discernible meaning, any written communication employing human language requires this.

Second, the first two thousand years of recorded history demonstrate that the literal grammatical historical hermeneutic was exclusively used. In the first twelve chapters of the Genesis narrative (a section of Scripture which covers roughly two

---

principle is no more circular in its reasoning than is the first-principle of any competing epistemological system.

[127] Proverbs 1:7.

[128] 1:2.

[129] 2:6.

[130] 9:10.

thousand years), we find some thirty-one occurrences of the phrases "God said," "the Lord God said," and "the Lord said." In all but possibly one instance the listener responds to God's word as if understanding God in the natural, normative way the employed language describes. The light comes into existence, just as God commanded.[131] Everything else during creation week employs the same hermeneutic. Even God Himself uses the literal grammatical historical hermeneutic: He describes how He will make man,[132] and then He does exactly what He said.[133] After the Fall, Adam and Eve still understand that God means exactly what He says, as they respond directly to His questions, understanding them through the same hermeneutic lens as before.[134] God gives Noah specific instruction, commanding him to build a precisely designed boat.[135] Thankfully, Noah did not employ an allegorical or spiritualized hermeneutic as he took God's words for what they were and did exactly what God had told him to do.[136] Finally, God told Abram to go,[137] and Abram did exactly as God told him.[138]

The only recorded exception to the two-thousand-year rule is found in 3:1, where the serpent challenges what God said. Even in this, the serpent doesn't specifically employ a different hermeneutic method, but he does challenge the truth of what was said and God's motivation in saying it.[139] In short, the only

---

[131] Genesis 1:3.
[132] 1:26.
[133] 1:27.
[134] 3:9, 14.
[135] 6:14-21.
[136] 6:22.
[137] 12:1.
[138] 12:4.
[139] 3:4-5.

one who is recorded to have questioned or challenged God's meaning during the first two thousand years of history is the serpent. These chapters provide a clear indicator of how God intends to be understood, and underscore the difficulty encountered when the simple meaning of the communication is not followed. Based on at least these two evidences (linguistic and historical) the literal grammatical historical hermeneutic is *sine qua non* to a Biblical epistemology. Without simplicity and univocality in meaning, there can be no Biblical epistemology (at least not as Solomon describes it). Simply put, along with the other components of epistemology, the Bible prescribes a knowable and discernible hermeneutic method for its readers.[140]

Eschatological Implications of a Biblical Epistemology

Employing a Biblical epistemology, we can discern from Scripture a Biblical metaphysic. With respect to ontology, God the Father,[141] God the Son,[142] and God the Holy Spirit exist.[143]

---

[140] While there may be some later instances in which the NT writer re-tasked an OT passage, those instances do not alter the initial meaning. In Matthew 2:15, for example, the event described in Hosea 11:1 is newly revealed as a foreshadowing of Christ, but the clear statement of Hosea 11:1 still stands, and Israel is still the referent. It is important to realize that in such instances the NT writers are generally *using* the text, not reinterpreting it. However, even if in some instances there *actually were* redefinition, it would seem the prerogative of a Divine author to handle things as He so desires, but He never extends that prerogative to the interpreter, instead there is a clear and normative precedent for grammatical-historical understanding throughout the Biblical revelation.

[141] Ephesians 4:6.

[142] John 1:1, 1 Corinthians 8:6.

[143] Genesis 1:2, John 14:26.

Creation exists.[144] Mankind exists.[145] Angels exist.[146] Satan exists.[147] With respect to a Biblical teleology, all things are purposed simply for His glory.[148] With respect to axiology, ultimate value is not an intrinsic thing but rather an instrumental one, since it requires an Ultimate Valuer. Therefore, God's ultimate purpose has to be considered when trying to understand what is good. That which God declares is good, *is good*, and it seems He determines what is good based on how it contributes to His overall doxological purpose.[149]

The questions of ontology, teleology, and axiology provide relatively simple answers, because, in the case of ontology things either exist or they don't; in the case of teleology, there is much Biblical data on the ultimate purpose of all things; and in the case of axiology, value is simply determined by the teleology: that which God declares is good, is good for accomplishing the purpose of His glory, and is therefore good to Him – the Ultimate Valuer.

Eschatology is a bit unique in comparison to ontology and teleology, however, as the eschatological data is so voluminous, and considers so many prophetic events. The questions of eschatology are far more complex than those of ontology and teleology. Still, historically, eschatology has been distilled into three basic interpretive traditions: premillennialism, postmillennialism, and amillennialism. Advocates of postmillennialism and amillennialism continue to readily admit

---

[144] Genesis 1:1.
[145] Genesis 1:27.
[146] Genesis 19:1.
[147] Revelation 12:9.
[148] E.g., Numbers 14:21.
[149] E.g., Hebrews 13:21.

that their views are supported by the occasional use of non-literal hermeneutics.[150] Some, such as Kevin DeYoung, advocate for reading one's theological system into the text in order to support the views of that system. DeYoung questions rhetorically, "Without a systematic theology how can you begin to know what to do with the eschatology of Ezekiel or the sacramental language in John 6 or the psalmist's insistence that he is righteous and blameless?"[151] Likewise, critics of premillennialism admit, along with Louis Berkhof, that dispensational premillennialism is only defensible if a literal grammatical historical hermeneutic is employed.[152]

Still, it is evident that premillennialism is not *the foundational issue* in a Biblical worldview and is not even *the pivotal issue* in eschatology. Rather premillennialism is a metaphysics-category outworking of epistemology, ontology, teleology, and axiology. John Piper's optimistic premillennialism (similar to Covenant premillennialism),[153] for example, can still be classified as premillennialism, yet his sociopraxy includes a non-cessationist approach consistent with Daniel Fuller's

---

[150] E.g., Sam Storms, "Why I Changed My Mind on the Millennium" at http://thegospelcoalition.org/article/why-i-changed-my-mind-about-the-millennium.

[151] Kevin DeYoung, "Your Theological System Should Tell You How to Exegete" at http://thegospelcoalition.org/blogs/kevindeyoung/2012/02/23/your-theological-system-should-tell-you-how-to-exegete/.

[152] Louis Berkhof, *Systematic Theology*, 4th Revised and Enlarged Edition (Grand Rapids, MI: Eerdmans, 1941), 706-715.

[153] Matt Perman, "What does John Piper believe about dispensationalism, covenant theology, and new covenant theology?" at http://www.desiringgod.org/articles/what-does-john-piper-believe-about-dispensationalism-covenant-theology-and-new-covenant-theology.

revelational/non-revelational view on inerrancy,[154] and Wayne Grudem's more recent "middle ground"[155] non-cessationist approach that suggests that the gift of prophecy does not always result in inerrant declarations, and that even Biblical prophecy can sometimes be "a bit wrong."[156] Piper admits to being "significantly influenced" by Grudem's view.[157] This aspect of (ecclesiological) sociopraxy is incompatible with the foundational epistemological principles of a Biblical worldview, in that this particular brand of non-cessationism alleges essentially that there are incorrect statements in Biblical prophecy. Notably, Piper advocates testing NT prophecy to determine if it is "good."[158]

The point here is that one can draw a basic premillennial conclusion without building it on the Biblical epistemological basis, and that resulting aspects of sociopraxy (as in Fuller's, Grudem's, and Piper's case) will not necessarily be compatible with Biblical epistemological grounding. Consequently, premillennialism (or the lack thereof) is simply not the issue. *How premillennialism is arrived at is of central importance here.* Thus, it is fair to say that a Biblically derived premillennialism is a necessary outworking of a Biblical epistemology and a necessary condition for a Biblical sociopraxy. In other words, Biblically derived premillennialism is simply one

---

[154] Daniel Fuller, "Benjamin B. Warfield's View of Faith and History" in Evangelical Theological Society *Bulletin*, Vol. II, No. 2, Spring 1968: 80.

[155] Wayne Grudem, *The Gift of Prophecy in the New Testament and Today* (Wheaton, IL: Crossway, 2000), 17.

[156] Ibid., 79.

[157] John Piper "What is the Gift of Prophecy in the New Covenant" podcast, at http://www.desiringgod.org/blog/posts/piper-on-prophecy-and-tongues, 1:00.

[158] Ibid., 1:48.

domino in a long sequence of dominoes in a Biblical worldview. If premillennialism is Biblically derived,[159] it will carry with it key components unique to dispensational premillennialism that are foreign to Covenant and other forms of dispensational premillennialism, including the complete distinction between Israel and the church and the absence of the church in the Old Testament (OT). In short, Biblically derived premillennialism will cause other distinctive dominoes to fall.

Socio-Political Implications
Of a Biblically Derived Premillennialism

Having established a Biblical epistemology and the necessary connection between a Biblical epistemology and a Biblical metaphysic (including the elements of ontology, teleology, eschatology, and axiology), we have focused a bit more directly on premillennialism, as opposed to other eschatological principles. Moving from the is[160] category (including epistemology and metaphysics) to the ought[161] category (including praxeology or ethics, and sociopraxy or socio-political thought) we examine some of the implications of a Biblically derived premillennialism, as it pertains specifically to sociopraxy.

As mentioned at the outset, characterizations of dispensational premillennialism as a negative socio-political influence have included charges of pessimism and anti-Semitism. There are of course many other indictments against dispensational premillennialism, but these two are answered

---

[159] See Appendix II, for a summary of how premillennialism is supported by the Hebrew Prophets.
[160] Or, descriptive.
[161] Or, prescriptive.

here simply to demonstrate the internal cohesiveness of the Biblical worldview as it pertains to Biblically derived pre-millennialism.

Pessimism

It is certainly true that Biblical prophecy, literally understood, does not paint an optimistic picture for the future of the world: "...the earth and its works will be burned up."[162] Revelation adds that future events will include a third of all trees and grass being destroyed,[163] a third of all life in the sea dying,[164] a third of all freshwaters becoming toxic,[165] a third of the sun, moon, and stars being darkened.[166] If the interpreter is working from a Biblical epistemology, which requires a literal grammatical historical hermeneutic, the interpreter must acknowledge that these things are coming at some point in the future.

But there is a tremendous distinction between an eschatologically pessimistic metaphysic regarding the present form of the heavens and earth and a pessimistic sociopraxy. The question at issue is whether or not a so-called pessimistic metaphysic must necessarily result in a pessimistic praxeology and/or sociopraxy. The Bible answers this question in the negative. In fact, the coming negative events are cited by Biblical writers for the express purpose of calling believers to optimistic action.

---

[162] 2 Peter 3:10b.
[163] Revelation 8:7.
[164] 8:9.
[165] 8:11.
[166] 8:12.

Peter, after describing coming cataclysms and the restoration to follow, exhorts believers to look for these things and in the meantime to "be diligent to be found by Him in peace, spotless and blameless, and regard the patience of our Lord to be salvation..."[167] Earlier in the context Peter explains that the Lord's patience has to do with His "not wishing for any to perish but for all to come to repentance."[168] Likewise, the book of Revelation is addressed to the churches,[169] and includes multiple ethical and sociopraxical exhortations.[170] While Revelation does not provide any specific socio-political imperatives, Peter's writings do.

Despite what some might call metaphysic pessimism, Peter mandates that believers keep their behavior excellent so that those who observe will glorify God.[171] Peter calls on believers to be submissive to government and to treat all men with honor.[172] Finally, Peter asserts that the prophesied future is a basis for godliness and goodness.[173] Paul considers similar themes in Romans 12-13 and 2 Timothy 3. Rather than being pessimistic in his own actions and those he prescribes of others, Paul has a vigorous sense of urgency to serve well, to be faithful, and to be a benefit to all around him for the sake of their eternal good.[174]

In short, the Biblical pessimism about the imminent future is a basis for believers' selfless and beneficent conduct of

---

[167] 2 Peter 3:14-15a).
[168] 2 Peter 3:9.
[169] Revelation 22:16.
[170] E.g., 2:5, 2:10, 2:16, 2:25, 3:3, 3:18-20.
[171] 1 Peter 2:12.
[172] 2:12-17.
[173] E.g., 1 Peter 4.
[174] E.g., 1 Corinthians 9:14-23.

life, as believers anticipate the ultimate eternal future. Consequently, the criticism of Biblically derived premillennialism as promoting pessimistic praxeology and sociopraxy falls in the straw-man category of fallacies, as such allegations confuse the *is* with the *ought*. To illustrate, the ontological reality that it is highly likely that your ice cream will melt soon is not grounds for your pessimism. In fact, it is quite the opposite. It provides you with an urgency based in truth, and grounding for doing the right thing with the ice cream while you have the opportunity.

Anti-Semitism

Wilson's critique of dispensational premillennialism is likewise a conflating of *is* and *ought*, as he assumes that the prophetic expectation of anti-Semitism naturally leads to the sociopraxical tolerance of anti-Semitism. On the assertion that dispensationalism expects a future anti-Semitism, Wilson is correct. Revelation 12:13, in context, describes a Satanic effort to destroy the Jews. Clearly if Satan is leading that charge it would be odd that anyone would think the church would be complicit in such efforts. Yet, history does not lie in connecting the historical organization of the "church" with anti-Semitism. From Chrysostom's *Eight Homilies against the Jews* to Luther's *The Jews and Their Lies* to the comments of numerous popes, there is no shortage of historical material demonstrating the "church's" displeasure with the Jewish people. But the grand irony here is that it is not dispensational premillennialism, but reformed and replacement theology that is historically guilty of anti-Semitic tendencies.

Yes, dispensational premillennialism interprets literally passages like Matthew 23:31-36 (Jesus speaking), Acts 2:36

(Peter speaking), and 1 Thessalonians 2:14-16 (Paul speaking) –
passages which acknowledge that it was Jews who rejected
Jesus and ultimately had Him crucified. But the point cannot be
lost that during that same week when Jesus pronounced the
Jews guilty, He died to pay for the sins of Israel and Judah under
the terms of the New Covenant;[175] it was Peter who encouraged
those he indicted to change their minds about the Messiah, that
they might be forgiven,[176] and who later wrote to Jewish
believers wishing them "grace and peace" in the fullest
measure,[177] and recounting Jesus' sacrifice in terms similar to
Isaiah 53,[178] and so appealed to Jesus as the Jewish Messiah;
and it was Paul who wrote to the Thessalonian believers – a
church he founded by his preaching of the gospel to the Jewish
people,[179] and who proclaimed to the Romans that the good news
of God's revealed righteousness was to the Jew first and then the
Greek,[180] and that consequences for evil,[181] reward for doing
good,[182] and ultimately the good news of God's revealed
righteousness[183] was to the Jew first and then to the Greek. And
of course, all three men were Jewish. A literal reading of the text
(as is required by a Biblical epistemology, and which undergirds
Biblical eschatology and sociopraxy) allows absolutely no room
for anti-Semitism, nor advocates for any tolerance of it.

---

[175] Matthew 26:28.
[176] Acts 2:28.
[177] 1 Peter 1:3.
[178] 2:21-25.
[179] Acts 17:1-4.
[180] Romans 1:16.
[181] 2:9.
[182] 2:10.
[183] 1:16.

Conclusion

If hermeneutics is understood to be an integral component of epistemology, and if there is a knowable and discernible Biblical epistemology, then there is a knowable and discernible Biblical hermeneutic. If that hermeneutic is literal grammatical historical, and if premillennialism is an eschatological principle required by the literal grammatical historical model, then premillennialism is an eschatological principle required by a Biblical epistemology. Finally, if a Biblical model for sociopraxy is grounded in a Biblical epistemology, and if a Biblical worldview demands internal cohesiveness from its individual components, then the Biblical socio-political model must not contradict the epistemological principles upon which it stands.

Historically, Reformed epistemology departs from the syllogistic sequence above at the very first point. Cornelius Van Til illustrates the Reformed methodology of perceiving hermeneutics as separate from the epistemological discussion,[184] and this is the maneuver that allows for the occasional employment of non-literal hermeneutics. This is the maneuver that undergirds both the postmillennial and amillennial perspectives, and this is the maneuver that grounds the resulting socio-political systems.

In order to justify premillennialism, for example, we must attend to the epistemological grounding that supports it. In order to understand the implications of premillennialism, we must likewise consider the socio-political applications of the eschatological principle. In short, we must recognize that if dispensationalism is to have any explanatory value at all it must

---

[184] See Appendix III.

be representative of *the* Biblical worldview. Consequently, in our understanding of and development of dispensationalism, we cannot focus only on narrow categories out of sequence, but we must do the work required to discern a Biblical worldview which is Biblically derived, which is foundational in its sequence, which is internally cohesive, and which is comprehensive. Only then will the full weight of dispensationalism's explanatory value be felt.

APPENDIX I[185]

Epistemology is the study of knowledge and seeks to answer the question of how we can have knowledge and certainty. Metaphysics is the study of reality and responds to questions regarding whether there is anything beyond the physical or natural. While I have often spoken of these two as interdependent, I have also been outspoken regarding the priority of epistemology over metaphysics in the context of fields of inquiry. Some might conclude from that prioritization that I am a foundationalist.

Foundationalism is a theory of epistemic justification (particularly espoused by Aristotle, and later, Descartes) that demands that beliefs must be warranted, or based on some foundation (in contrast to, for example, coherentism, which simply requires that a belief be coherent with a set of other coherently fitting beliefs in order to be justified). In prioritizing epistemology over metaphysics as a field of inquiry, I am not

---

[185] Adapted from Christopher Cone, "Which Comes First, Metaphysics or Epistemology" viewed at http://www.drcone.com/2014/04/02/which-comes-first-metaphysics-or-epistemology/.

drawing a foundationalist conclusion, but I am carefully qualifying the context of that prioritization.

Clearly, if we are considering the realm of reality, or asking about what actually exists, then metaphysics comes first. Reality comes before the questioning of that reality. What exists, exists, and whether it is questioned or not has no bearing at all on its existence. So, in the realm of what actually is, metaphysics comes first. However, in the context of human inquiry, we are seeking to understand what actually is. Metaphysics cannot come first in this context, because we have to have a reason to prefer one explanation to another.

This is not to draw a foundationalist conclusion, for example, that the existence of God must be justified in order to be true. On the contrary. God's existence has nothing to do with whether or not He can be explained or whether or not His existence is warranted. He either exists or He doesn't. But human inquiry in this area is the pursuit of understanding what is true. Does He exist or doesn't He?

Various epistemological models justify their conclusions in different ways. Humean empiricism says He doesn't exist because He has not been (and presumably cannot be) sensed. Cartesian rationalism reasons to His existence from the first assumption that He doesn't exist. But the Biblical model describes the fear of the Lord as the beginning of wisdom.[186] Consequently, the Biblical epistemology assumes the Biblical God's existence at the outset and works from that premise. That He exists comes first – that is the metaphysical actuality.

Metaphysically speaking, that I understand He exists comes after. But how I come to understand He exists is the

---

[186] Proverbs 1:7, 9:10.

epistemological question that I must first answer before I can support the metaphysical supposition and know whether or not that supposition is certain or correct. Metaphysics (the reality) comes first in actuality, but epistemology (how we can answer the question of what is reality) comes first in inquiry. Before I can derive answers in any field of inquiry, I must have some basis for preferring some answers to others. That is the epistemological question. My preferring some answers to others has no bearing on the actual legitimacy of those answers, but is an important reflection on the source of authority upon which I rely.

For a Biblicist, that source of authority is the Bible. According to the Bible, that God exists is the metaphysical reality[187] – and that comes first in the realm of actuality. At the same time, the Bible also asserts epistemic truth regarding how we can have knowledge and certainty – by the fear of (right perspective of and response to) the Lord.[188] The epistemic proposition is simply that knowledge begins with the acknowledgment of Him. For the purposes of our inquiry, we are given, as first principle, the means whereby we can have certainty of knowledge. In other words, in the realm of the human pursuit of wisdom and knowledge, the epistemic question comes first (how can we have wisdom and knowledge?) and is answered with metaphysical reality (by the fear of the Lord).

---

[187] Genesis 1:1.

[188] Proverbs 1:7, 9:10.

APPENDIX II

The Premillennial Anticipation in the Hebrew Prophets

The Hebrew prophets anticipated (as they were told by God) that God would come to earth and rule over Israel as a representative in the Davidic line. Dispensational premillennialism has long understood Revelation 19-20 as a narrative of the fulfillment of those promises and has been criticized by some for that understanding. The following discussion simply considers the anticipation of the Hebrew prophets regarding this future kingdom, as their prophecies form the contextual backdrop for the events of Revelation 19-20.

Isaiah 9:6-7

The Prince of Peace is both man (child, son, 9:6) and God (*el gabor*, Mighty God, 9:6). His government will be unlimited in increase and peace, and He will sit on the throne of David (9:7), to arrange or direct (*lehaqiyn*) it. This will be accomplished by the zeal of Yahweh Sabaoth. The establishment of the kingdom seems, in simplest terms, to be accomplished by this Messiah (or by Yahweh Sabaoth), and not by human agency (i.e., not by Israel or the church). Further, this kingdom is a literal kingdom in which this Messiah rules over the throne of David – David's kingdom was not a spiritual one, but a literal kingdom over Israel, centered primarily in Jerusalem.

Jeremiah 23:5-6

This prophecy speaks of a future time when a righteous branch will be raised for David (or on behalf of David), who will be a righteous king in the land of Israel (23:5). During His reign Judah and Israel will enjoy salvation and security, and He will be called Yahweh Tsidiqenu (The Lord our righteousness) (23:6). Considering the elements of this prophecy, the Lord will be a righteous king in the line of David, and in the land of David, consolidating the two kingdoms and bringing peace and security.

Jeremiah 30:7-9

Anticipating the great day of Jacob's trouble (30:7), this prophecy adds that Israel will no longer be under the yoke of others (30:8), but will serve God and David their king, who will be raised up for Israel (30:9). Here is yet another prophecy of national judgment and restoration, with the latter condition coming at a time when a Davidic king is ruling.

Jeremiah 33:15-26

A righteous branch of David (in this case, not David himself) is raised, and who executes justice and righteousness (33:15). Judah and Jerusalem will be saved during the administration of Yahweh Tsidiqenu (33:16). The enduring Davidic Kingdom (33:17) includes a Levitical priesthood (specifically the Zadokian line discussed in Ezek 40:46, 43:19, 44:15, and 48:11) (33:18). These things will take place as surely as the continuation of night and day (33:20-26).

Ezekiel 20:30-49

In a prophecy addressing the house of Israel directly (20:30), Adonai Yahweh declares that He will be king over Israel. He describes a physical regathering (20:34), a judgment (20:35-36), and an enacting of a covenant with Israel (20:37). This prophecy concludes with a call to action for that present generation of Israel, in light of the future rule of Yahweh Adonai from His holy mountain (e.g., 20:40). Ezekiel laments in the final verse that his listeners ignored the calls to action and considered the prophecy to be non-literal (20:49). It is evident from this prophecy that God intends to rule, literally, over Israel, in an economy governed by a covenant, and from His high mountain. In this context the regathering, the judgment, and the covenant all precede the ruling. Further it is notable that a non-literal understanding is explicitly frowned on.

Ezekiel 37:21-27

This prophecy begins with anticipation of a regathering (37:21) into the land of Israel, and the formerly separated kingdoms of North and South will be united under one king (37:22). David is referenced as king over them (37:24), and is also identified as their prince (37:25). David's status as king and prince (either in person or as representative of a royal line) does not invalidate earlier promises that God Himself would be king (e.g., 20:33). Associated with this rule is the establishing of a covenant of peace with Israel, a regathering, and a future with God present (37:26-27).

Daniel 2:34-35

The stone uncut by human hands first appears (2:34a), then strikes the feet mixed with iron and clay (2:34b), and then as the statue crumbles to dust, the stone grows to fill the whole earth (2:35). This sequential aspect is supported by the use of the vavs preceding the verbs for striking and filling. Simply put, the King appears, conquers the preceding kingdom, and then begins His rule. One could argue that the fifth kingdom begins with the striking of the fourth, but inarguably the stone actually appears before striking the statue and before filling the whole earth. This passage anticipates a pre-rule appearance of the fifth kingdom's King.

Daniel 9:24-27

The first verse in this pericope anticipates seven developments (to finish the transgression, to make an end of sin, to make atonement for iniquity, to bring in everlasting righteousness, to seal up vision and prophecy, and to anoint the holy of holies) during an allotted time sequence (i.e., seventy sevens). The sequence continues in verse 26 with Messiah being cut off after sixty-nine weeks, and desolations determined until the desolation of the Roman prince (who is to come) who makes and violates a seven-year covenant. There is no mention of a kingdom installed up to the point of that final desolation. If the destruction of the city refers to 70AD, then one who supports the view that the kingdom was somehow inaugurated with the advent of the church in 33AD must defend how times of desolations can be concurrent with the glorious rule of the Messiah. Gabriel's prediction here does not explicitly anticipate premillennialism, but it creates grand problems for the competing views of amillennialism and postmillennialism.

Zechariah 14:1-9

A day is coming in which what was taken from Israel will be returned (14:1). God Himself will gather the nations against Jerusalem, but ultimately God will *go forth* and fight against those nations (14:2-4). This will be a literal going forth, as He will stand on the Mount of Olives – changing its topography, and God will come with all the holy ones with Him (14:4-5). These events ultimately conclude with Yahweh as king over all the earth (14:9).

Conclusion

These are some passages that overtly anticipate God's kingdom coming to earth in physical, literal manifestation in the line of David, to rule not only over Israel, but also over the whole earth. In each case, the theme is the same: a regathering, judgment, and restoration of Israel under a Davidic king, who is ultimately God Himself. There is no textual reason at all to assume any of these references are to be understood in a non-literal way. In fact, the only time we see a non-literal response, that response is lamented.[189] From these passages it is evident that God would come to earth, in the Davidic line – appearing first, then meting out judgment and restoration, then ruling as king. These nine passages all support the premillennial coming of the Messiah, even if the details regarding the first segment of that kingdom as lasting one thousand years are not revealed until later.[190]

Louis Berkhof famously criticized premillennialism, suggesting that "the Scriptural basis for this theory is Rev. 20:1-6, after an Old Testament meaning has been poured into it."[191] Despite Berkhof's criticism, it should be expected that in these final passages of Scripture the promises God made would be fulfilled. If Revelation 19-20 does not represent the fulfillment of these numerous and similar prophecies, then what would? Berkhof adds, "This passage occurs in a highly symbolic book and is admittedly very obscure...The literal interpretation of this passage...leads to a view that finds no support elsewhere in

---

[189] Ezekiel 20:49.

[190] Revelation 20:2-7.

[191] Louis Berkhof, *Systematic Theology*, 4th Revised and Enlarged Edition (Grand Rapids, MI: Eerdmans, 1941), 715.

Scripture."[192] This author suggests that the literal interpretation of Revelation 19-20 is not at all obscure or symbolic and is fully supported by each of the nine Hebrew prophecies discussed above.

APPENDIX III[193]

Cornelius Van Til is brilliant on what I would call the first three pillars of Biblical epistemology (#1: Biblical God exists, #2: He has revealed himself authoritatively, #3: Natural man's incapacity to receive), but his epistemology falls short in that he does not account for hermeneutics (Pillar #4) within his epistemology. In fact, in his Th.M thesis, "Reformed Epistemology," he never once even discusses Biblical interpretation. Much of his critique of other thinkers, like Kant, includes considerable discussion of their deficiencies in the interpretation of experience, but not a word about interpretation of Scripture. Not one.

How can Van Til build such an outstanding foundational framework on special revelation and then totally ignore the centrality of hermeneutic method for understanding that revelation? You see, it all has to do with where one places hermeneutics: Biblical hermeneutics is as an absolutely necessary component of epistemology. Hermeneutics falls within the realm of epistemology. Van Til does not seem to share that conviction, even though he critiques the hermeneutics of others'

---

[192] Ibid.

[193] Adapted from Christopher Cone, "Two Deficiencies of Reformed Epistemology" viewed at http://www.drcone.com/2014/04/28/two-deficiencies-of-reformed-epistemology-a-brief-commendation-and-critique-of-cornelius-van-tils-epistemology/.

bases of authority (i.e., experience) within an epistemological context.

Still, while not considering hermeneutics an integral part of epistemology, he does give hermeneutics attention elsewhere. In his *The New Hermeneutic*, for example, Van Til concludes, with these words, "...we would appeal to the Cahier's men, to Wiersinga and to others, to build their hermeneutical procedures on the theology of Calvin, Kuyper, Bavinck, etc., (emphasis mine) and then in terms of it to challenge all men to repentance and faith in the self-identifying Christ of Scripture instead of making compromise with unbelief" (pp. 180). Notice his prescribed hermeneutical procedures are grounded in historical theology, rather than literal grammatical historical.

In short, Van Til is marvelously consistent in his epistemological method until he arrives at the hermeneutic component. At that point his writing shows, in my estimation, two deficiencies: (1) he does not grant hermeneutics its proper and necessary place in epistemology, and (2) when he does consider hermeneutics, he prescribes historical theology as the orthodox hermeneutic, rather than literal grammatical historical – an unfortunate contradiction of his own expertly stated first principles. The Biblical epistemological model does not share these two deficiencies and leads me to consider that while Van Til is outstanding up to a point, we cannot simply adopt his reformed epistemology without ourselves walking more consistently down the reformed path. Premillennialism (and especially the dispensational form of premillennialism) demands its own epistemology, and one that includes hermeneutic method.

CHAPTER 4

THREE VIEWS ON THE KINGDOM: IMMINENT, ALREADY NOT YET, AND NOT YET

How one views the kingdom of God has significant implications on one's ethical and socio-political perspectives. For those who acknowledge that the kingdom of God is a significant reality, there are three popular views on the timing of the kingdom: (1) The view that the kingdom was imminent when Jesus announced it, (2) the view that it is both already here and not yet here, and (3) that it is not yet here.

THE IMMINENT VIEW

Popularized by Johannes Weiss and Albert Schweitzer, Schweitzer called the *Imminent* view *consequente Eschatologie*, meaning consistent or thoroughgoing eschatology. In Weiss's *Die Predigt Jesu vom Reiche Gottes (Proclamation of the Kingdom of God)* (1892) he presented Jesus as proclaiming the kingdom in an apocalyptic[194] manner, expecting it imminently during His lifetime rather than through a gradual building of

---

[194] The label *apocalyptic* refers to eschatological writings that include a view to the consummation of all things.

the kingdom by human labors and morality. Likewise, Albert Schweitzer's *The Mystery of the Kingdom of God* (1901) understood Jesus's teachings to advocate an imminent supernatural only kingdom. What Weiss theorized, Schweitzer popularized.

In this understanding, ethics was not the way into the kingdom – repentance was. Schweitzer understood the Sermon on the Mount to represent an interim ethic. For Schweitzer, the kingdom was imminent, supernatural, and apocalyptic. It was not an internal spiritual reality, but rather an imminent supernatural reality. Because Jesus's kingdom *didn't* come, according to Weiss and Schweitzer, they understood Jesus to be wrong in His eschatology. Nonetheless, Schweitzer still viewed Jesus as dying for the sins of humanity and legitimately calling people to follow his humanitarian goodness.

For Weiss and Schweitzer, that Jesus was not eschatologically reliable is not of great importance as Jesus still provided a worthy moral example, at the very least.

THE ALREADY NOT YET VIEW

C. H. Dodd advocated for a realized eschatology – the idea that Jesus was not presenting the kingdom as future, but as a present reality here and now. George Eldon Ladd tried to balance out Dodd's realized eschatology with an acknowledgment that there was a still yet future component of the kingdom. Ladd's was an *already not yet* eschatology. Ladd perceived that the Scriptures contain a "bewildering diversity of statements about the Kingdom of God,"[195] and he resolves what he perceives to be contradictory ideas by merging two major interpretations. He suggests, "The Word of God *does* say that the Kingdom of God is a present spiritual reality,"[196] citing Romans 14:17, which reads, "for the kingdom of God is not eating and drinking, but righteousness and peace and joy in the Holy Spirit." Alluding to that same passage, he later describes the kingdom as "an inner spiritual redemptive blessing."[197] Ladd notes, "our Lord describes those who received His message and mission as those who *now* enter into the Kingdom of God,"[198] citing Luke 16:16, which records that "The Law and the Prophets *were proclaimed* until John; since that time the gospel of the kingdom of God has been preached, and everyone is forcing his way into it."

On the other hand, he admits, "At the same time, the Kingdom of God is a future realm which we must enter when Christ returns,"[199] citing 2 Peter 1:11, in which Peter suggests that "in this way the entrance into the eternal kingdom of our Lord and Savior Jesus Christ will be abundantly supplied to you." In these contexts, Ladd relies on the present tense to argue *not just timing, but also location*:

> The parables of the Kingdom make it clear that in some sense, the Kingdom is present and at work in the world. The Kingdom of God *is* like a tiny seed which becomes a

---

[195] George Eldon Ladd, *The Gospel of the Kingdom* (Grand Rapids, MI: Eerdmans, 1959), 16.
[196] Ibid.
[197] Ibid., 18.
[198] Ibid., 17.
[199] Ibid.

great tree; it *is* like leaven which will one day have permeated the entire bowl of dough (Luke 13:18-21). Yet on the other hand, when Pilate examined Jesus about His teaching, Jesus replied, "My kingdom is not of this world" (John 18:36).[200]

Similar to Ladd, D. Martyn Lloyd-Jones asserts,

It is a kingdom which is to come, yes. But it is also a kingdom which has come. 'The kingdom of God is among you' and 'within you'; the kingdom of God is in every true Christian. He reigns in the Church when she acknowledges Him truly. The kingdom has come, the kingdom is coming, the kingdom is yet to come. Now we must always bear that in mind. Whenever Christ is enthroned as King, the kingdom of God is come, so that, while we cannot say that He is ruling over all in the world at the present time, He is certainly ruling in that way in the hearts and lives of all His people.[201]

For Lloyd-Jones, there is a future coming kingdom, but the kingdom has also already come, residing in the hearts of believers.

Progressive Dispensationalists like Darrell Bock build this foundation of already not yet. Bock suggests that, "covenant theologians of the past have tended to overemphasize the 'already' in their critiques of dispensationalism, while

---

200 Ibid., 19.
201 D. Martin Lloyd-Jones, *Studies in the Sermon on the Mount* (Grand Rapids, MI: Eerdmans, 2000), 16.

underemphasizing the 'not yet.'"[202] Like Bock, D.A. Carson, observes that, "the kingdom came with Jesus and his preaching and miracles, it came with his death and resurrection, and it will come at the end of the age."[203]

With the kingdom already here, there is an aspect of spiritualizing some aspects of the kingdom in similar fashion to postmillennialism (the view that Jesus returns after the kingdom is established) and amillennialism (the view that there is no literal kingdom. In each of these views, the church bears ultimate responsibility for ensuring the kingdom of God is established on earth.

THE NOT YET VIEW

The *Not Yet* view, recognizes that the kingdom of God is currently only a heavenly kingdom (hence the constant Matthean references to the "kingdom of the heavens"), and that it will one day come to earth in a literal, physical form as was preannounced in the Davidic Covenant of 2 Samuel 7. The fulfillment of that promise begins in Revelation 20, with Jesus's sitting on the throne in Jerusalem and reigning for one thousand years. This view relies on the literal grammatical historical method for understanding the prophecies pertaining to the kingdom.

John Darby notes that what is presently on earth is in contrast to the kingdom and is in no way a fulfillment. He suggests, "In fact we know John was beheaded, and the Lord was

---

[202] Darrell Bock, "The Reign of the Lord Christ," in *Dispensationalism, Israel, and the Church* (Grand Rapids, MI: Zondervan, 1992), 46.
[203] D. A. Carson, *Matthew, Expositor's Bible Commentary,* Vol. 2 (Grand Rapids, MI: Zondervan, 1995), 101.

crucified, and the kingdom presented in Him, and by Him, was rejected by Israel. By-and-by it will be set up visibly and in power. Meanwhile the church is set up, because the kingdom is not set up in this manifested way."[204] Stanley Toussaint agrees with Darby's understanding, and asserts that Matthew 13:11 does not refer to "a kingdom in the so-called 'mystery form'"[205] Toussaint adds, "The kingdom exists [now] only in the sense that the sons of the kingdom are present. But strictly speaking the kingdom of the heavens in Matthew 13 refers to the prophesied and coming kingdom on the earth."[206]

Also holding to this idea, Charles Ryrie notes that, "Because the King was rejected, the Messianic, Davidic kingdom was (from a human viewpoint) postponed. Though He never ceases to be King and, of course, is King today as always, Christ is never designated as King of the church...Though Christ is a King today, He does not rule as King. This awaits His second coming. Then the Davidic kingdom will be realized (Matt. 25:31; Rev. 19:15; 20)."[207] While disagreeing with the *Not Yet* view, even Covenantalist theologian Louis Berkhof recognizes that dispensational teaching claims that "the church has nothing in common with the Kingdom."[208] As Berkhof suggests, in a literal grammatical historical understanding of the NT, the kingdom is not here and now.

---

[204] J.N. Darby, *Collected Writings* (Addison, IL: Bible Truth Publishers, 1972), 25:47.

[205] Stanley Toussaint, *Behold the King* (Grand Rapids, MI: Kregel, 1980), 172.

[206] Ibid.

[207] Charles Ryrie, *Basic Theology* (Chicago, IL: Victor Books, 1986), 259.

[208] Louis Berkhof, *Systematic Theology* (Grand Rapids, MI: Eerdmans, 1941), 710.

Matthew's support of this view is significant, since he references the kingdom directly in his gospel at least fifty-one times, which account for nearly a third of all NT references to the kingdom.[209] A literal understanding of the references in Acts[210] also supports the view. The Pauline Epistles[211] likewise support the *Not Yet* view, when understood with the literal grammatical historical hermeneutic. James,[212] Peter,[213] and John[214] likewise present the kingdom as *only* an earthly reality in the future.

IMPLICATIONS

These three eschatological views have hermeneutical implications, as how one understands the related passages largely determines the theological outcome, and the theological outcome sets the course for believers' understanding of ethical responsibility and socio-political stewardships.

First, the *Imminent* view denies literal grammatical historical hermeneutics and treats *some* of Jesus's teaching as non-authoritative. The *Imminent* view represents Jesus as eschatologically incorrect, but morally correct. It would be fair

---

[209] 3:2; 4:17,23; 5:3, 10, 19-20; 6:10, 13, 33; 7:21; 8:11-12; 9:35; 10:7,11; 11:12; 12:28; 13:11, 19, 24, 31, 33, 38, 41, 43-45, 47, 52; 16:19, 28; 18:1, 3-4, 23; 19:12, 14, 23-24; 20:1, 21; 21:31, 43; 22:2; 23:13; 24:14; 25:1, 34; 26:29.

[210] 1:3, 6; 8:12; 14:22; 19:8; 20:25; 28:23, 31.

[211] Romans 14:17; 1 Corinthians 4:20; 6:9-10; 15:24, 50; Galatians 5:21; Ephesians 5:5; Colossians 1:13 (which is a pivotal passage), and 4:11; 1 Thessalonians 2:12; 2 Thessalonians 1:5; and 2 Timothy 4:1, 18.

[212] James 2:5.

[213] 2 Peter 1:11.

[214] Revelation 1:6, 9; 5:10; 11:15; 12:10.

to ask that if Jesus can be so wrong in some areas, how can we trust Him in others?

The *Already Not Yet* view is arbitrary in its hermeneutics, ultimately disputing the principle of single meaning. Further, the *Already Not Yet* view brings the church into Israel's promises, by failing to distinguish between the promised kingdom of heaven in 2 Samuel 7 and Matthew 3-26 and Christ's present heavenly kingdom, spoken of in Colossians 1:13. *Geography matters.*

In contrast to these two views, the *Not Yet* view is the only view of the three that is consistent in its application of literal grammatical historical hermeneutics. The *Not Yet* view is also the only view of the three that recognizes a distinction between the promised kingdom of heaven in 2 Samuel 7 and Matthew 3-26 and Christ's present heavenly kingdom, spoken of in Colossians 1:13. Finally, the *Not Yet* view is the only view of the three that maintains the complete distinction between Israel and the church, and thus is the only one that avoids entirely replacement theology.

How the kingdom of God is constructed determines a great deal about the Christian's place in socio-political responsibility. It is thus a foundational component of a truly Biblical approach to a just society, and hence, social justice. While very little has been said beyond merely introducing the three views, their examination is worthwhile, as their advocates build on these theological foundations with disparate practical conclusions.

CHAPTER 5

THREE VIEWS ON LAW AND ETHICS: CONTINUITY, SEMI-CONTINUITY, AND DISCONTINUITY

Romans 6-7 and Galatians 2-6 have much to say about the role of law (and *the Law)* in ethics and society. How we understand the function of law – and the Mosaic Law, specifically – goes a long way toward helping us determine our understanding of individual and societal ethics. Three views in particular have helped shape contemporary understanding of Biblical ethics and socio-political thought. The Continuity view holds that the entire Law of Moses is still in effect and applicable to believers today. The Semi-Continuity view asserts that portions, but not all of the Law are in effect and applicable. The Discontinuity view suggests that the Law of Moses is entirely fulfilled and is not a governing model for today.

Before we can arrive at a well-earned conclusion regarding which of these views is most valid, we need to consider the very nature of good and God's relationship to good.

THREE MODELS FOR UNDERSTANDING GOOD

Illustrated by Plato's *Euthyphro,* Socrates questions the young Euthyphro on the nature of good and asks an important question: whether good is good because the gods prefer it, or whether the gods prefer good because *it is* good. In other words, is good arbitrary (and thus is merely good because the gods fancy it), or is it absolute (in which case the gods *must* prefer it because it is good)?

In moving the discussion away from the Greek pantheon and considering it in more Biblical terms, we discover that there are three prevailing perspectives on goodness and God's relationship to good. First, the view that that which is truly holy is that which is loved by God. In this view, God is under good – He is subject to the absolute principle of good. This view places the ideal of authority under law itself.

The second view considers that God is an example of holiness (or vice versa). He does not define good; He is simply an example of it. Likewise, law comes from Him as an outworking of His character. (This view is similar to Euthyphro's assertion that what he is doing [in accusing his father of murder] is good – when Socrates asks Euthyphro for a definition of good, Euthyphro can only offer him an example.) In this view, God is good, and authority is law itself.

The third view asserts that God defines what is good and is thus over good. In this view authority is over law. That which is loved by God is holy – because He loves it. His valuation *makes* it holy. One could say that the establishment of value is based on the valuation of the Chief Valuer.

The first view has a fatal flaw: it places God under good, and He is obligated to act in a certain manner. In this view, *good* is God, and God is just the middleman. The second view also has a fatal flaw, in that it offers no definition of good. God is merely the prime example of good. The third view suffers no such flaw, but it can appear undesirable to some, as some have perceived this to be the might-makes-right principle – whoever has the power gets to set definitions, whether they are just or not. I would argue that might-makes-right is not at all accurate or sufficient. On the other hand, absolute-might-makes-right would be a much better (more Biblical) model. Because God is the Creator and thus Sovereign over His creation, He gets to determine and define. Just because one has power does not give them the right to determine and define, but One who has absolute power – and rightly so – indeed has the authority to determine and define.

Interestingly, these three understandings of the nature of good and God's relationship to it set the tone for how we understand law, ethics, and social justice. Further, the three understandings are very evident in perspectives on law and the Mosaic Law and their role in all of this.

THE CONTINUITY VIEW

The *Continuity* view suggests that the Law of Moses continues in full today and is applicable not only to believers, but also to society as a whole. Advocates of this view suggest that the Law can be divided into three parts – the moral, civil, and ceremonial. All three parts are applicable today. This view is rooted in a strong form of the authority-is-law concept – the view of good that says God is good, providing an example, but no definition. Because of the reliance on authority-is-law, if the authority doesn't change, then neither can the law. Greg Bahnsen, a notable Theonomist, refers to this as "the abiding validity of the Law,"[215] and suggests that Matthew 5:17 makes it clear that the moral, civil, and ceremonial components are still applicable. If God doesn't change and He is the authority, then His law can't change either. If His law can't change, then it cannot be fulfilled but must still be in effect. If law is simply an expression of His character, then all of His law must remain unchanged. Like James said, if one violates one aspect of law, that one has violated the entire law.[216]

There is some inconsistency here as the ceremonial law is perceived as simply restorative, and thus once restoration has occurred, then that aspect is fulfilled. Bahnsen suggests that, "The accomplishment of redemption changes the way in which we observe the ceremonial law, and the change of culture and times alters the specific ways in which we observe the case laws. The cases are different, but the same moral principles remain."[217] Without Bahnsen's caveat or one similar, advocates of this view would be faced with the thorny issue of requiring ongoing sacrifices despite the Hebrews 7:27 admonition that there has been one sacrifice for all.

Theonomy and Reconstructionism are two applications of the *Continuity* view. In these applications, the Law of Moses should be the governing law for society and should be enforced by force if necessary. Interestingly, this is the same basic view of good and law that undergirds Islamic socio-political thought.

---

[215] Greg Bahnsen, *Theonomy in Christian Ethics* (Nacogdoches, TX: Covenant Media Press, 2002), Chapter 2.
[216] James 2:10.
[217] Greg Bahnsen, "The Faculty Discussion of Theonomy," Question 9, http://www.cmfnow.com/articles/pe192.htm, 1978, at RTS.

THE SEMI-CONTINUITY VIEW

The *Semi-Continuity* (SC) view suggests that the Law of Moses continues in part today, is applicable to believers for their ongoing growth (sanctification), and is a model to society as a whole. Like the *Continuity* view, SC divides the Law of Moses into three parts but recognizes only the moral law (the Ten Commandments) as broadly applicable today. In this view the civil and ceremonial aspects of the Law have been fulfilled. Acts 15 shows the ceremonial law to not be applicable to believers, and several NT writers voice their approval (or at least tolerance) of non-theocratic governmental authorities,[218] thus rendering the civil law aspect of Moses' Law nonapplicable today. The moral law, on the other hand is still necessary for personal growth and sanctification.[219] Samuel Bolton suggests that, "The law sends us to the gospel that we may be justified, and the gospel sends us to the law again to enquire what is our duty in being justified."[220]

Like the *Continuity* view, SC works from the authority-is-law platform but in perhaps a slightly weakened iteration. God is good, and His character and legislation reflect that goodness. While holding to the idea that God doesn't change, there is a recognition that His Law can change. In this metaphysical premise the *Continuity* view is more consistent than SC, though they both have problems fulfilling the James 2:10 standard. David Jones faces a dilemma when he says,

---

[218] E.g., Romans 13:1-5, 1 Peter 2:13-17.
[219] David Jones, *Introduction to Biblical Ethics* (Nashville: TN, B&H Academic, 2013), 139.
[220] Samuel Bolton, *True Bonds of Christian Freedom* (London: UK, Banner of Truth, 1964), 80.

"Since the Decalogue is a reflection of God's moral character, the norms codified in the Ten Commandments are universally applicable and demonstrable both before and after their issuance on Mount Sinai."[221] This is an acknowledgement of the authority-is-law metaphysic and of the need for a consistent application. Jones adds that this has socio-political implications: "As the kingdom of God grows, then the gospel gradually counteracts and corrects the effects of sin in the world through the process of restoration and reconciliation...the gospel is no less comprehensive than the fall..."[222] The problem arises in the application of these stated principles. Notice how the application of the Sabbath is changed for the contemporary audience:

> For Christians, then, the Sabbath is a sign of redemption and, as such, it depicts the eternal rest they have received from Jesus in salvation...Keeping the Sabbath ought not to be a legalistic burden, characterized by lists of permitted and forbidden activities. Rather the Sabbath ought to be a joyous celebration and a blessing...In a specific sense the fourth commandment calls believers to observe a regular day of worship...not to observe the Sabbath, in either a broad or a specific sense, is to behave in a distinctly un-Christlike manner...in the NT...the early church moved the day of Sabbath observance to the first day of the week.[223]

The inconsistency is in the reinterpreting of the Sabbath while asserting it is not being reinterpreted. The Sabbath most

---

[221] Jones, 139.
[222] Jones, 64.
[223] Jones, 166.

certainly *was* a legalistic burden. It was mandated by law, and restricted all manner of accesses and behavior. Further, in no sense does it call believers to observe a regular day of worship – the Sabbath was not a day of worship, it was a day of *rest.* Further, it is not correct to state that the early church moved the day of Sabbath observance to the first day of the week. The meeting of the body of Christ and the Sabbath had nothing whatsoever to do with one another. This reinterpreting allows the SC advocate to maintain the metaphysical premise, but it is not sound exegesis.

Reformed and Covenant theology in general hold to the SC view, recognizing current applicability of certain aspects of Mosaic Law, and expecting societal adaptation to that law, either by legislative pressures or by force (as has been the case in some historical settings). Jones underscores the influence of this view when he calls it "the prevailing view of the church."[224]

It is not only Reformed and Covenant thinkers, however, who hold to the SC view, but also those who might hold to a form of dispensational thought but prefer to employ Covenantalist methodology and metaphysical presuppositions. For example, John MacArthur echoes the SC premise when he notes that, "the big picture way to understand it is this: God's law is a manifestation of His nature. What God has commanded, moral attitudes and behaviors, is a reflection of His nature."[225] Once the metaphysic premise is established, it becomes a theological necessity:

---

[224] Jones, 76.
[225] John MacArthur, https://www.gty.org/library/sermons-library/GTY164/sanctification-sin-and-obedience.

So, to come along and say that the law is unimportant is to say that the very nature of God and the will of God as reflected in His law is insignificant and unimportant, which I see as a blow or a strike against the very character of God. That is why, at the end of Romans 3, Paul says, after talking about justification by grace through faith alone, he says, "Do we nullify the law?" And then he says, *me genoito*, "No, no, no, God forbid: but we establish the law."[226]

Once the theological necessity is established, the practical implications are apparent. The Law is now part of the believer's sanctification – and inevitably societal regulation:

And that new nature is a new, divinely created disposition infused with power from the Holy Spirit so that you can now, for the first time, actually obey the law. And not just obey the law, but love to obey the law.[227]

This new relationship to the Law allows us to live in conformity with the Law of God:

...salvation is both a forensic reality – that is, God declares you righteous by imputing His righteousness to you – and it is also a real change so that you now are given the ability to live righteously, which is to live in conformity to the law of God and do so willingly from the heart.

---

[226] MacArthur, Ibid.
[227] MacArthur, Ibid.

MacArthur is careful to say that believers aren't under the Law for salvation: "...when Paul says you're not under the law, he first means you're not under the law as a means of salvation."[228] but it is clear that in his model, believers *are under law,* being saved so that they can live in conformity with the Law, and do so willingly and lovingly. So, while the metaphysical and hermeneutic methodology of Covenant theology is a primary factor in the development of the SC view, the view and its requisite implications are held by some even outside of that doctrinal family.

THE DISCONTINUITY VIEW

The *Discontinuity* view differs from the other two views in that it (exegetically) *must* recognize that authority is *over* law, thus God is over His law, and can change or fulfill it as He desires. Because of this key metaphysical premise, God could fulfill the Mosaic Law through the death of Christ,[229] rendering it non-applicable for the believer's sanctification and as a societal governor without compromising His own character and consistency. In this view, there is no exegetical warrant nor theological need to subdivide the Law of Moses into three categories, as the entire covenant has been fulfilled in Christ. Of course, the Law (and law – or ethics – in general) is still vitally important as it serves as a tutor to lead people to Christ,[230] but it is not a regulatory device any longer. *Discontinuity* recognizes

---

[228] MacArthur, Ibid.
[229] Ephesians 2:15.
[230] Galatians 3:24-25.

a single ethical standard: the holiness of God.[231] The holiness of God undergirds distinct ethical mandates for unbelievers and believers.

For unbelievers, there is a universal vertical accountability to God for falling short of His holiness.[232] There is also a universal mandate to respect the sanctity of human life because of the *imago dei* in every human being.[233] This adds a horizontal aspect – a socio-political responsibility for unbelievers not to murder others. Then there is the redemptive mandate for unbelievers to become believers in Him. The nature of all unbelievers is irreparably marred, as we were all children of wrath, living in the deadness of sin.[234] It is evident there is no ethical quality or redemptive power outside of faith.[235] Finally, the condition of remedying this condition is simply by faith in Him.[236]

For believers, the vertical accountability to God has been resolved, as we have been justified by faith. Once the position is established, the practice is expected. Believers should be obedient by being holy.[237] Believers should be holy by loving God.[238] Further, believers love God by being obedient.[239] It is evident that holiness, obedience, and love are all intimately connected and, in some respects, interchangeable. Holiness, obedience, and love are expressed in specific ways, both vertical

---

[231] 1 Peter 1:15.
[232] Romans 1:18-21, 3:23, Matthew 5:48.
[233] Genesis 9:6.
[234] Ephesians 2:1-3.
[235] Hebrews 11:6
[236] Genesis 15:6, Habakkuk 2:4, John 6:47, 20:27-31.
[237] 1 Peter 1:14-16.
[238] Matthew 22:37-40, 1 Corinthians 16:22.
[239] John 14:15, 21, 24, 15:10, 1 John 5:2-3.

(toward God), and horizontal (toward others). Regarding the horizontal aspect, there remains the universal sanctity of life mandate. There is a requirement to love other believers,[240] seeking for their benefit and ultimately their sanctification.[241] There is a requirement to love unbelievers,[242] seeking their benefit and ultimately their justification.[243]

The *Discontinuity* view is more Biblically agreeable than the other two views in that (1) it follows from a Biblical epistemology, rooted in the literal grammatical historical hermeneutic, and (2) it follows from Biblical metaphysics – that God is holy (ontology), that God determines good (axiology), that all is for God's glory (teleology), and that God will be glorified (eschatology). The *Discontinuity* view is also more preferable in its practicality than the other two views in that it (1) provides certainty even in difficult ethical situations, (2) allows for clarity in Biblical ethical and socio-political contexts, and (3) leads to specific socio-political thinking compatible with the ideas advocated in these chapters, and which have undergirded freedom and advancement in society.

---

[240] Matthew 22:37-40, John 13:34-35, 15:12-13, 1 John 4:7, 5:2.
[241] Galatians 6:10, Philippians 2:3-5, Hebrews 10:24.
[242] Matthew 22:37-40, 5:44, Luke 10:29-37, Romans 12:19-21, 1 Corinthians 5:9-13, Colossians 4:5-6, 2 Timothy 2:24.
[243] John 3:16, Galatians 6:10, Ephesians 2:3-7, Philippians 1:15-18.

CHAPTER 6

THE ESSENTIAL EQUALITY OF WOMAN

By Christopher and Catherine Cone

Let us consider the identity of *woman.* Who is she? She is created in God's image. We start in Genesis 1:26-28. "God said let Us make man in Our image according to Our likeness. Let them rule over the fish of the sea, the birds in the sky, over the cattle, over all the earth, over every creeping thing that creeps on the earth. God created man in His own image. In the image of God, He created them; male and female He created them."[244] First, we need to understand that humanity was originally designed to rule. It wasn't just designed for man to rule, it was intended that both of them would rule. They are identified collectively as man and woman, as humanity. They were designed to be co-regents. That was the plan described in Genesis 1.

Notice that "God created man in His own image, in the image of God He created him. Male and female, He created them."[245] The plural pronoun is used indicating that they are created *man and woman* and created in the image of God.

---

[244] Genesis 1:26-28.
[245] 1:27.

Essential equality is the starting place. If the reader has any doubts about who they are, they can be encouraged in the knowledge that God starts with identifying who they are. Their identity, each individual's identity, starts with Him and His design.

In the summative description of His creation, all is declared to be *good*. God saw all He had made and this summative statement concludes the whole discussion of creation: "And He saw all that had been made, and behold it was very good."[246] There's an emphatic statement in the word *behold*. It was abundantly good.

In chapter two we see the lens zooming in to tell us about how woman was created. In verse eighteen we get the first instance in all of recorded history of something being *not good*. Notice verse eighteen. "Then the Lord God said, 'It is not good for the man to be alone; I will make him a help suitable for him.'"[247] As we have a recounting of this creation event, there's something incomplete about it. It's not good because Adam is alone. The man is alone, and in verses nineteen and twenty God shows him his need. So, He brings many animals before Adam and shows him they all have pairs, but he doesn't. It's just him. God shows Adam his need, and then God meets that need. Notice in verse eighteen it says that she will be a help. In verse eighteen as God announces what He's going to do, He says He's going to make *a help*. Not a helper (though some translations read that way), but a help. This is the same term used in Hosea 13:9 referring to God. As God is talking to Israel, He says "you are rejecting your Lord, your help." Some women may read this

---

[246] Genesis 1:31.
[247] 2:18.

passage and say "you know I I'm not interested in being a helper. That is not who I am." Perhaps some might perceive it as demeaning. It isn't at all. Think about what God is saying in Hosea 13:9. *He* is the help. So, when He creates an entire gender to be the help, this is an awesome thing. Unfortunately, we have a pretty pathetic view of help these days, and we need to change that. In this passage, however, we see why God created woman and what His plan was. We see this aspect of woman's identity, that while made in God's image she is designed to complete this incredible creation that God had accomplished.

In verse twenty-two we see that Adam was made out of dirt. His name actually is the word for *dirt*. Red dirt, more specifically. Woman, however, is fashioned. A different verb is used. She is built, not simply created out of dust. It's pretty interesting that God does something aesthetically very different with the woman than he did for the man.

Let's think about equality of woman. In Galatians 3:28 we see that man and woman are together *one* in Christ Jesus. Male and female is not the relevant issue here. There is a unity in Christ Jesus. We see in 1 Peter 3:7 that we are fellow heirs. 1 Peter 3:7 says, "and show her honor as a fellow heir of the grace of life."[248] She is a fellow heir, or co-heir. In Matthew 19:4 and Mark 10:6, Jesus is talking. He reminds that from the beginning He made them male and female. Woman is not an afterthought. There is a design; there is a purpose and a process. Before He created woman, He wanted to show man the need. That is significant.

In 1 Corinthians 11:8 we discover the aspect of equality and interdependence. Here, man does not originate from woman

---

[248] 1 Peter 3:7.

but woman from man. It was recorded in Genesis 2 that the woman was built from the rib of Adam. In 1 Corinthians 11:9, "for indeed man was not created for the woman's sake, but woman for the man's sake." This is similar to what we read in Hosea 13:9, where God was functioning for Israel's sake. Notice in 1 Corinthians 11:11-12, "however, in the Lord, neither is woman independent of man, nor is man independent of woman. For as the woman originates from the man, so also the man through the woman; and all things originate from God." In other words, there is this incredible interdependence with man and woman. By the way, it is not simply talking about marriage here. Humanity is male and female, and it is evident how the two need each other.

Ephesians 1 is a passage which talks about how the Father, Son, and Spirit all work to save believers. Man and woman are one in the body of Christ. God is very active and engaged with both male and female, denoting that there is essentially equality. It is within our essence that we are made in the image of God, where we are equal in the sight of God. We are fellow heirs, co-heirs.

Let's talk about the character of women. There are a few passages which highlight this. First Timothy 2 highlights a couple of aspects. In verse nine, Timothy has just talked about how men are to engage. This is all in the context of the local assembly, in the church. He says in verse nine, "likewise women to adorn themselves with proper clothing, modestly and discreetly, not with braided hair and gold or pearls or costly garments."[249] Some use a passage like this to say, "so you obviously can't braid your hair." But context is incredibly

---

[249] 1 Timothy 2:9.

important, right? Verse ten continues, "but rather by means of good works."[250] In other words, he is not talking about what the person is wearing (go outside clothed with just your good works, and you will probably get arrested!). He is talking about that which truly adorns a person. The word *cosmetic* comes from the Greek word (*cosmos*),[251] which means *proper or order*. It identifies the same principle we see in Matthew 5-7 in the sermon on the mount, as Jesus is proclaiming to His audience. He is explaining to them that entrance into His kingdom is not about external righteousness or obedience to the Law, but a kind of internal character is necessary. What He is telling those Jewish individuals there in Matthew 5-7 is they don't have that character – specifically, the righteousness God requires to get into the kingdom. Jesus was speaking to change their minds about how they get into the kingdom and explain to them that righteousness is not about external. It is about the internal. Of course, Whom is the source of that internal righteousness? Christ Himself. So, He is setting up His entire earthy ministry in those chapters. In the same way, it is the *character, or righteousness* of the woman that is to adorn her. It is about the inside, the internal, not the external. That is what Paul is saying here. If he was saying you cannot wear braids, then verse ten would be saying you can only wear good works (let us not go any further with that). There is a similar thing presented in 1 Peter 3:3-4. It is about internal character. And, by the way, we are just talking about women here, but for men it is very, very similar. That's why we look at Matthew 5:37. It is because Jesus is talking to men and women telling them it is not about external

---

[250] 1 Timothy 2:10.
[251] 2:9.

righteousness. It is about internal character, internal righteousness. Especially in our culture it is a great challenge for men and women, especially for women, regarding appearances and the external. So much focus is put on that. As Paul reminds us, we ought not let that be our adornment. That is not what is important.

How about the ministry of women? Now, this is interesting. This list is nowhere near complete, but here are just a few of the areas that we see women encouraged to minister: as wives, as mothers, as providers, as nurturers, as teachers, as disciplers. We see all of them. Women are crafted to minister at home first – so are men by the way. Men are crafted to minister at home first. We have gotten this so misaligned in our culture that somehow the man should focus on activities outside the home, and the woman should focus on those inside the home. That is a disastrous way of thinking, and not at all what the Bible represents.

There is another thing that we need to focus on, and we see it in 1 Timothy 5:1. "Do not sharply rebuke an older man, but rather appeal to him as a father." It is interesting that it starts with a home relationship. Paul continues, "to the younger men as brothers," He uses family and home language, right? He continues, "The older women as mothers."[252] Well, what if they are not mothers? Appeal to them as if they are your mothers. If you are having a discussion with an older woman, consider her as your mother. Treat her with honor and respect. Treat "the younger women as sisters."[253] Then there is this concept thrown in at the end: "in all purity."[254] The point in reading these verses

---

[252] 1 Timothy 5:2.
[253] 5:2.
[254] 5:2.

is that all men and women are identified and characterized by these familial relationships. Our culture is so broken and our definitions of families have become so scattered, that we think any reference to the nuclear family must somehow be archaic. This is what God has designed. It is how He has made us. It is how He has designed us. We are to treat each other this way. So, when we see that women are crafted to minister at home first, it is not any different for men, and it is an absolutely glorious thing.

How about 1 Timothy 5:14? This one is especially pointed in some translations, saying that "she is to keep house," and that doesn't sound really great, right? That sounds like she is cleaning counters and sweeping floors and that is as far as women can minister in this age, as if that is the primary task of women. That is, of course, not the case. The term Paul uses here is really interesting. You have heard the term *despot*. A despot is a ruler, a lord, a manager, and in this context an *oikodespoto*[255] is one who is managing, leading the house, running it. So, in this context Paul is explaining that women are to be managing the house. Now this is not headship, but it is certainly management and supervision. We do not talk about that very much if at all.

A couple of verses later we see that if any woman who is a believer has family who are widows, it is her job to assist them so the church isn't burdened. She is to provide for widows in the family. So, she is also a provider there.

We can also say that women are crafted for marriage. We see that in Genesis 2. That is the design. Women are crafted for marriage, but not *only* for marriage. We could also say that men

---

[255] 1 Timothy 5:14.

are also crafted for marriage. We see the same thing described of men in Genesis 2. Men are crafted for marriage in general. Women are crafted for marriage in general, but *not only* for marriage. 1 Corinthians 7 is a really helpful passage in this regard. In verses two through seven Paul describes how marriage is designed to keep humanity from immorality. One of the things discussed in this context is that in marriage neither person is their own. He describes how the wife belongs to her husband and the husband belongs to his wife. In verse six, He says, "but this I say by way of concession not of command."[256] In other words, marriage isn't a command. He is saying marriage is helpful in these ways, but then he also says if you can stay single that is even better. So, it is not a command to get married. If you are not married it is not a deficiency. Paul is explaining to the Corinthian church that if they can be single, they can be more focused on what the Lord is doing, because he talks about these various challenges of life. Now, if you find someone who is as focused on the Lord as you are, then marriage can be an incredible thing. It can help you be more focused and have accountability, encouragement, and strengthening, but God hasn't provided that for everybody. In verses seven and eight we see that Paul calls celibacy a gift. "Yet I wish that all men were even as I myself am. However, each man has his own gift from God, one in this manner, and another in that."[257] So, if you are not married, that is a gift from God. If you are married, that is also a gift that God has given you. What Paul is saying is: *enjoy your gift*. Appreciate it and walk in that path. Marriage is a big part of this. Women are designed and equipped to be wives but

---

[256] 1 Corinthians 7:6.
[257] 7:7.

that is not all they can or should be. And if they are not married, they have a different gift, but a gift nonetheless.

Considering Titus 2:3-5, we see an aspect of women's ministry in *teaching*. Paul says that women are to be teachers. He is talking to older women, telling them to be good teachers of younger women so that these younger women can become who they are supposed to be. They can understand who they are and what their ministry is. Of course, for the man *and* for the woman, their ministries are largely but not exclusively home centered. Older women are to teach younger women. So, we see that discipleship aspect, that nurturing aspect. Colossians 3:16 describes how all believers are teaching and admonishing one another. So, *every woman is a teacher* and is designed and even advocated to be teaching. A practical question for women might be: are you a good teacher, are you teaching the right things? Another question is, who are you teaching and in what context? Women are designed to be teachers.

We have a portrait of the excellent woman in Proverbs 31:10-31. We see a few characteristics in verses ten through twelve. We see she is good for her husband. She is a great blessing to him. We see that as a manager she delights in providing for those in her care. In verse sixteen she considers a vineyard, buys it, and plants. She is running this industry as part of her being a wife. In verses seventeen through nineteen she is very diligent, night and day. In verse twenty she cares for the poor, not just in an unconnected way, but actually providing for them directly. In verses twenty-one through twenty-two she clothes her family and herself, in that order. It is worth noting that in this context Solomon describes this woman as being well clothed. Going back to what Paul says about the external adornment, he is not saying you cannot braid your hair. He is saying that is not what makes you beautiful, but this woman is making the very most out of what she has for her family and for herself. In verse twenty-three her husband is well esteemed because of her efforts. In this context he is respected not because of himself but because of her. It has been said that behind every great man is a woman rolling her eyes. That is not what this is talking about here. He is esteemed because of who she is.

Verse twenty-four describes how she engages in business. She is an incredible woman of high capacity. This is an excellent woman. In verse twenty-five she is adorned with strength and dignity, and she is unafraid. We should all love to be like this person, like this excellent woman because she is *excellent in her character, adorned with strength and dignity, and unafraid.* In verse twenty-six she teaches wisdom and kindness. (Are we teaching wisdom and kindness?) She fulfills in verse twenty-seven her home-centered stewardship diligently. Notice it is not all exclusively home focused. There is a home-centered stewardship, and in this context, she is fulfilling it very, very diligently. She is faithful. Verses twenty-eight through thirty show that she prioritizes properly. She is commended for her walk with the Lord. She is then commended by her husband and blessed by her children. That is really awesome because her report card is coming from God primarily, then from her husband, and then from her children. So, she is praiseworthy and she is praised. Now, there is a lot of responsibility for husbands and children that come out of these passages as well. How do you treat an excellent woman? Guys this is a big deal. If you do not know how to treat an excellent woman, you must learn – this is part of being a praiseworthy man. This woman is praiseworthy and she is praised.

Let us talk about marriage. There are a couple of central passages to think through. Ephesians 5:22 says, "Wives be subject to your own husbands." Except, there is no verb in verse twenty-two. There is no "be subject" in verse twenty-two. Going back to verse twenty-one, we need to ask to whom is Paul talking? To all believers. "Be subject"[258] is the Greek *hupotasso,* to align oneself under each other in the fear of Christ. In other words, we are accountable to Him. It is similar to what he says in Philippians 2 about considering the other as worthy of more honor than ourselves. In Ephesians 5:22 and following, Paul begins to explain what that looks like in each of the home relationships and in those beyond the home. In verse twenty-two he says, "wives to your own husbands as to the Lord." In other words, there is a special kind of *hupotasso* or under alignment. It is a military term signifying a willing alignment of oneself under someone else. Wives are reminded to align themselves under *as if to the Lord.* In fact, this is not about the husband at all. In verses thirty-one and thirty-two we are reminded of Genesis 2 and what marriage was created to be. After quoting Genesis 2 we read in Ephesians 5:32, "this mystery is great; but I am speaking with reference to Christ and the church." So, the overarching aspect here is that God created marriage as an illustration of the relationship that Christ would have with this church about four thousand years in the future. That is awesome! And as we walk through this passage in Ephesians, we discover that the wife is called to illustrate the role of the church. She is to be responsive to her husband as the church is to be responsive to Christ. It is a beautiful portrait of what the relationship is supposed to look like. Of course, the husband, on

---

[258] Ephesians 5:21.

the other side, is supposed to illustrate the role of Christ loving His own bride and giving Himself up for her, totally self-sacrificial for her spiritual well-being. The wife's role is not dependent on the husband and the husband's is not dependent on the wife. These are not conditional commands. In fact, when we get to 1 Peter 3, we discover there are great consequences to all of this. First of all, in 1 Peter 3:8-9, we see that all are to be godly. So, once again we have that *universal church* language. All are to be godly. 1 Peter 3:1-2 tells wives to be submissive. This is our translation: *even if your husbands are idiots*—so they can be won without a word. The wife's responsibility has nothing to do with the man, and the husband's responsibility has nothing to do with the woman. They are accountable to God to fulfill these roles so that all the world can see what Christ's love for His church and the church's response to Christ's love looks like. It is supposed to be everywhere there is marriage. This love of Christ is supposed to be evident. But of course, it often doesn't happen.

First Peter 3:7 highlights the importance of this aspect of relationship: "You husbands in the same way, live with your wives in an understanding way." And then it says, "as with someone weaker." You have heard women referred to as the weaker sex. This is not at all what the Bible is representing here. This is a comparative. It is urging the man to be gentle with her as if she were weaker. It is not saying she is weaker, it is a comparative. "Since she is a woman; show her honor as a fellow heir of the grace of life."[259] Hermeneutics is a big deal. How we handle the text is a big deal. If we get these essential truths of our identity wrong, we will completely misunderstand who God

---

[259] 1 Peter 3:7.

has made us to be. Beyond that, we misunderstand who God is, and we start treating each other wrongly. We do harm. We are destructive. What does God think of that? Notice the end of verse seven as Peter is talking to these husbands. If you do this wrong, your prayers will be hindered. Does God always answer prayer? Not if a man is not living with his wife in an understanding way. That is what Peter is telling husbands here. That is a big deal. So, our walk with the Lord is impacted by how we are engaging with each other. It is a big deal. This is not conditional. This is not "I will take you for my wife as long as you are who you seem to be today", or "I will take you for my husband as long as you seem to be who you are today." This commitment is not conditional and is quite a responsibility. But there are a couple of sticky passages beyond this.

Let us talk about some boundaries. First of all, everybody has them. Men and women have boundaries and limitations. There are things that are inappropriate for men and things that are inappropriate for women because of God's picture, the portrait, the design, what He is intending to illustrate. The basic limitation is: portray the roles that God has designed for you, and do not step into roles He has designed for others. That principal fits across every aspect of life. Going back to 1 Timothy 2:11, Paul states, "A woman must quietly receive instruction with entire submissiveness. But I do not allow a woman to teach or exercise authority over a man, but to remain quiet." This is another instance where context is really important. We call this the pastoral letter, the first of three pastoral letters because Paul is telling Timothy what the function of the church ought to look like, and he is explaining here what the conduct of man and woman ought to be like in the church. Remember, just like in marriage there are roles, pictures, that are being illustrated.

Paul explains that it is based on the order of creation that a woman is not designed to teach or lead men in the church setting. In verse fourteen he says, "And it was not Adam who was deceived, but the woman being deceived, fell into transgression."[260] And then some translations use the plural, "But *women* will be preserved through the bearing of children if *they* continue in faith and love and sanctity with self-restraint."[261] If we do not handle this passage well, we have women being saved for their eternal salvation by bearing children. Is that what Paul is talking about here? Of course not. That would be nonsensical. There is not a plural here. In fact, the term is a singular, "but she will be preserved or saved through the bearing of a child." We would suggest the child-bearing is a reference to Eve. She was looking for this child who would be born, who would be the Redeemer, the promised Deliverer, from Genesis 3:15. This passage paints a clear limitation. Just like in the marital construct, the man is portraying something and the woman is also. If we do not get those portrayals right in a marriage, the marriage is not functioning in our Creator's design.

We see the same thing in the church. The context that Paul is describing, of the function of the local churches painting a picture, we also see in 1 Corinthians 11:15. This whole discussion about a woman's hair and praying with her head uncovered or covered is in that context. Here is the punchline to all that. Verse fifteen says her *hair is given to her as a covering*. The woman is not required to wear a separate covering. Her hair is given to her for that purpose, and it illustrates her being under

---

[260] 1 Timothy 2:14.
[261] 2:15.

the headship of Christ overall, and it signifies the headship of the man over the woman, as he is portraying the role of Christ and His church. Obviously, this concept can be and has been abused, but headship is evident in this passage. Importantly, it is not conditional upon the quality of the man or the quality of the woman. Our identity is found in Christ, and we play roles in life that illustrate aspects of that identity. We have designs to fulfill. In 1 Corinthians 14, this is one of the reasons we see there is a limitation on women and the use of revelatory and prophetic gifts in the assembly. Some will pull that out of context and say it means she cannot talk at all, total silence. He is talking specifically about prophesying in tongues within the context of the local church in that age. So, there are boundaries – for both men and women – and we need to understand them.

Finally, let us look at some exemplary women. In Luke 23:49 women are a vital part of Jesus' early ministry. They are accompanying Him the whole time. In Acts 1:14 there are women at the very beginning in the upper room waiting for the coming of the Holy Spirit. In Acts 9:36 we are introduced to a lady named Tabatha who is an awesome godly person. In Acts 16:13-15, we are introduced to Lydia, a businesswoman, a leading woman. She comes to Christ and does some incredible things. In Acts 17:4, leading women are part of the founding of the church there. In Acts 18:2 and 26, we see Priscilla and her husband Aquilla. She is named first, and they are even teaching an individual about the Holy Spirit. Romans 16 names a number of faithful women. Philippians 4:2-3 talks about Euodia and Syntyche, two leading women in the church who are who are phenomenal women, but they are not getting along. He encourages them to get along. In 2 Timothy 1:5 we are told about Timothy's mother Eunice and his grandmother Lois – an awesome woman of faith. Hebrews 11 tells of more women of faith: Sarah, Rahab, and many others, some who are described as being sawn in two, people of whom this world was not worthy.

So, who are you? These are just a few examples from the NT, but, women, *who are you?* You are a woman designed to glorify Him. You are created in Christ Jesus for good works which He prepared beforehand so that you would walk in them. You have been bought by your Savior for a price, and it is not your life; it is His. So, allow Him to be glorified in all that you do. Be the beautiful and amazing woman that He designed you to be. If you do not think you are important, and your design is important, and your identity is important, think about the first attack ever on humanity. It was on the woman, on who she was and what God had intended for her. That's a big deal.

Precious Lord, we are so grateful for you. We love you. We thank you and praise you for all that you have done and how you have designed us. You crafted us and made us. We are grateful. We pray that we will find our identity in you, understanding what you have designed for us, understanding that your ways are greater than ours, and your perspective is greater than ours. Help us Lord to fulfill your design. Help us to encourage one another and build one another up and truly treat one another as worthy of more honor than ourselves. Help us to encourage each other in the lofty design you have for each of us. We love you.

CHAPTER 7
ADDRESSING LGBTQ:
A BIBLICAL TELEOLOGICAL ARGUMENT
FOR IDENTITY, SEX, AND SEXUALITY[262]

Matthew Vines and others supporting the LGBTQ perspective have argued for a *Moral Permissive View* on sexual orientation. The argument has been two-tiered: (1) that the more traditional *Moral Prohibitive View* is based on six Scriptures that are ultimately not relevant to the present discussion, and (2) that in the absence of Biblical data for or against healthy homosexual relationships, Christians should choose the more inclusive, affirming approach rather than condemn such relationships.

In order to advance the discussion beyond the stalemate of these two models, and in order to apply a solidly Biblical hermeneutic, this paper proposes a third approach: *The Inherent Design Model.* This third model considers God's particular design for identity, sex, and sexuality in Genesis 1 and 2, Jesus' affirmation of that model in Matthew 19, Paul's recognition in 1 Corinthians 7 that the design offers only one

---

[262] Originally presented to the Bible Faculty Summit, International Baptist College and Seminary, Chandler, Arizona, August 7, 2019.

inherent alternative (celibacy), and his explanation in Romans 1 of other alternatives as violating God's design. The *Inherent Design Model* concludes that LGBTQ applications violate God's design, and the model contextualizes the ethical implications so that believers can respond in a way that honors all people (including LGBTQ), and can demonstrate the love of Christ while not compromising Biblical truth.

INTRODUCTION

In a 2014 episode of the TV series Blue Bloods, a dialogue between a reporter and the series' Catholic lead character, NYPD Commissioner Frank Reagan, drew attention to the perception of the RCC's stance on same-sex relationships:

> *Reporter: The Catholic Church condemns homosexuality as a sin and the Commissioner is famously Catholic. How do you line up your anti-gay faith with your role as an equal-opportunity employer?*
> *Reagan: What my men and women do in private is their own business.*
> *Reporter: So you only condemn homosexuality on a Sunday?*
> *Reagan: Well, I do believe that the Church is a little behind the times on this, but then I still miss the Latin Mass.*[263]

---

[263] Blue Bloods, "Burning Bridges ," Directed by John Behring, Written by Willie Reale, CBS, October 10, 2014.

While numerous commentators disagreed with the show's representation of the RCC view of homosexuality,[264] the dialogue illustrated the friction present even among the most ardent followers regarding issues related to same-sex relationships. What once was a din has now become a crescendo of public opinion that the Judeo-Christian model for sexuality is no longer correct or beneficial.

The Barna Group reports that "the decades-old trend that Christianity is irrelevant is giving way to the notion that Christianity is bad for society."[265] More than eighty percent of adults in the US believe it is very or somewhat extreme to refuse to serve someone because the customer's lifestyle conflicts with their beliefs. Between fifty and seventy-nine percent believe it is very or somewhat extreme to believe that sexual relationships between people of the same sex are morally wrong. The same percentage perceives it to be equally extreme to teach children that sexual relationships between people of the same sex are morally wrong.[266] The increasing divide between culture and Christianity is perhaps more evident in the area of same-sex relationships than in any other context. Just as same-sex advocates have been active in trying to expose the disconnect,

---

[264] E.g., Jane Chastain, "Blue Bloods Has People of Faith Seeing Red," JaneChastain.com, October 15, 2014, viewed at https://janechastain.com/2014/10/15/blood-bloods-has-people-of-faith-seeing-red/, and Susan E. Wills, "Blue Bloods" Blooper Exposes Confusion about the Church and Gays," Aletia.org, October 12, 2014, viewed at https://aleteia.org/2014/10/12/blue-bloods-blooper-exposes-confusion-about-the-church-and-gays/.
[265] The Barna Group, "Five Ways Christianity is Increasingly Viewed as Extremist," Barna.com, February 23, 2015, viewed at https://www.barna.com/research/five-ways-christianity-is-increasingly-viewed-as-extremist/.
[266] Ibid.

the Christian community has engaged the issue, but has neither been definitive nor particularly effective in holding back the groundswell. In 2003, for example, twelve percent of Protestants considered same-sex relationships to be morally acceptable, up to fifteen percent in 2013. Among Catholics the 2003 number was nineteen percent, and nearly doubled to thirty-seven percent in 2013. In both groups a growing minority approves of same-sex relationships, while those who associate with no faith approve homosexuality at a rate of seventy-one percent.[267] As faith is perceived to be increasingly irrelevant, it is fairly clear that the trend toward acceptance of same-sex relationships will continue.

Among Evangelicals there are two prominent arguments, one for and one against the morality and acceptability of same-sex relationships. The Moral Permissive View, proposed by advocates of homosexuality and supported by a cultural distance argument, postulates that because there are no explicit prohibitions in the NT, the overwhelmingly negative mood toward homosexuality is cultural and is specifically targeting inappropriate homosexual activity and is not addressing committed and monogamous homosexual. On the other hand, in more traditional Evangelical circles, the longstanding Moral Prohibitive perspective abides, supported by legal restrictions in the Mosaic Law that are presupposed and uncontradicted in the NT and thus remain applicable for today.

This writer suggests that a third approach, an Inherent Design View, provides a superior argument, in that it (1) is more

---

[267] The Barna Group, "America's Change of Mind on Same-Sex Marriage and LGBTQ Rights," Barna.com, July 3, 2013, viewed at https://www.barna.com/research/americas-change-of-mind-on-same-sex-marriage-and-lgbtq-rights/.

methodologically consistent with a literal grammatical historical approach to the Scriptures, (2) draws exegetically justifiable conclusions about the character of God and the origin of morality, and (3) recognizes the progress of revelation allowing for both a cogency and discontinuity in God's revelation on the matter. If the Inherent Design approach accurately represents the Biblical record, then readers can have confidence even if the Biblical record itself is contrary to current streams of prevailing culture. In that case, the solution would not be found in conforming the Bible to culture (as does the Moral Permissive View), nor in condemning culture based on Mosaic norms (as does the Moral Prohibitive View), but rather in recognizing the Creator as the Sovereign and Designer, to Whom we should look for our identity, definition, and purpose.

In any consideration of such matters of great controversy, it is appropriate to remember why we are engaging the discussion in the first place. Paul provides an important preface to such discussions when he reminds Timothy that "the goal of our instruction is love from a pure heart and a good conscience and a sincere faith."[268] The discussion, rightly engaged, ought to produce an expression of Christlike love that is rooted in purity, goodness, and sincerity. In other words, love is the vital conclusion – not love in a general sense, but rather a certain kind of love – a prescribed kind of love designed by our Creator for accomplishing His purposes. As we compare the merits and limitations of these three perspectives, we are reminded that there is no room for hatred of or disrespect toward people,[269] nor

---

[268] 1 Timothy 1:5. Unless otherwise indicated, all Scripture references are from the NASB, copyright by the Lockman Foundation.
[269] 1 Peter 2:17.

is there room for compromising truth,[270] lest we show hatred of and disrespect toward our Creator.

MORAL PERMISSIVE VIEW
(CULTURAL DISTANCE THEOLOGY)

Built on the essential yet unstated premise that God cannot or will not hold a person morally accountable for what they do not choose, Matthew Vines asserts that "Gay people have a natural, permanent orientation toward those of the same sex. It is not something they choose, and it's not something they can change. They aren't abandoning or rejecting heterosexuality – that's never an option for them to begin with."[271] Vines adds an emotional appeal, emphasizing the hurt caused by viewing homosexuality as wrong:

Being different is no crime. Being gay is not a sin. And for a gay person to desire and pursue love and marriage and family is no more selfish or sinful than when a straight person desires and pursues the very same things. The Song of Songs tells us that King Solomon's wedding day was "the day his heart rejoiced." To deny to a small minority of people, not just a wedding day, but a lifetime of love and commitment and family is to inflict on them a devastating level of hurt and anguish.[272]

---

[270] Ephesians 4:15.
[271] Matthew Vines, "The Gay Debate: The Bible and Homosexuality," March 10, 2012, viewed at https://www.youtube.com/watch?v=ezQjNJUSraY.
[272] Ibid.

Elsewhere, Vines characterizes Paul's negativity toward homosexual activity as targeting only a particular kind of behavior. Vines suggests that, "Paul is explicit that the same-sex behavior in this passage is motivated by lust. His description is similar to the common ancient idea that people "exchange" opposite-sex for same-sex relations because they are driven by out-of-control desire, not because they have a different sexual orientation."[273]

Vines' advocacy of permissiveness is rooted in three key factors. First, Vines appeals to cultural distance – the idea that the culture that the Bible is addressing in its negative connotations of homosexuality is not the responsible culture of same-sex love that Vines seeks to exonerate. Second, God has an obligation to respect human free will, and can not (or will not) judge humanity for that which is not chosen. Finally, Vines' strongest and perhaps most effective appeal is to the heartache that he purports is brought on by condemnations of same-sex relationships. *Note that the desired outcome for Vines is not merely tolerance, but rather acceptance. Anything less will not resolve a devastating level of hurt and anguish.* Vines' argument is rhetorically powerful. Who would want to cause hurt and anguish? Certainly, no one who holds to any kind of Christian ethic. However, claims of injury of this sort are difficult if not impossible to prove, and they don't make for strong arguments, outside of their emotional appeal. Vines' other two premises, on the other hand, are perhaps more grounded in historic philosophical argument.

---

[273] Matthew Vines, "Debating Bible Verses on Homosexuality," New York Times, June 8, 2015, viewed at https://www.nytimes.com/interactive/2015/06/05/us/samesex-scriptures.html.

The idea that homosexuality is not a choice and thus cannot be condemned on moral grounds cuts to the heart of whether or not humanity is a completely free moral agent. While there has not, as of yet been provided any scientific data to suggest that homosexuality is actually individually predetermined, determinism is important to Vines' argument. The premise holds that if God were to judge that which is not chosen, then His justice could be questioned. But the flaw in this assumption is especially apparent in Romans 5. In that context, Paul acknowledges that Adam's sin resulted in the sinfulness of all humanity.[274] Thus, people who did not choose to be born were brought into this life, born into death and separation from God. They did not individually *first* choose against God, they were already by nature children of wrath,[275] enemies of God,[276] and helpless.[277] God holds humanity morally accountable for what they don't choose. Consequently, even if the claim that homosexuality is inherited and not chosen was demonstrated to be true, that would not invalidate God's sovereign right to hold His creation accountable on His own terms.

Vines' cultural distance premise is well voiced by Justin Cannon, who suggests that the Bible isn't addressing a culture of honorable and respectful homosexuality, but rather an abusive form of same-sex activity:

>...the Bible really does not fully address the topic of homosexuality. Jesus never talked about it. The prophets

---

[274] Romans 5:12-19 states six times explicitly that Adam's sin caused all to be in sin.

[275] Ephesians 2:3.

[276] Romans 5:8-10.

[277] Romans 5:6.

never talked about it. In Sodom homosexual activity is mentioned within the context of rape (raping angels nonetheless), and in Romans 1:24-27 we find it mentioned within the context of idolatry (Baal worship) involving lust and dishonorable passions. 1 Corinthians 6:9 and 1 Timothy 1:10 talk about homosexual activity in the context of prostitution and possibly pederasty. Nowhere does the Bible talk about a loving and committed homosexual relationship.[278]

In one sense, Cannon is right – there is minimal Biblical discussion of homosexuality compared to other issues. There are six clear references to same-sex activity in Scripture,[279] and yet there are forty-four mentions of adultery, thirty-five references to lust, seventy-two instances of deceit, and thirty-eight instances of jealousy. If the Scripture has so little to say on the matter, why the controversy? Cannon suggests that the six same-sex references are generally mishandled (by those advocating the Moral Prohibitive View), even with respect to the terminology used.

Raymond Hays helps interlocutors understand the significance of the terms chosen and argues that the verbiage is clear enough to invalidate the cultural distance premise. Hays' comments in that regard are worth noting here:

---

[278] Justin Cannon, "The Bible, Christianity and Homosexuality," GayChurch.org, viewed at https://www.gaychurch.org/homosexuality-and-the-bible/the-bible-christianity-and-homosexuality/.
[279] Genesis 19, Leviticus 18:22, 20:13, Romans 1, 1 Corinthians 6:9, and 1 Timothy 1:10.

The word *malakoi* is not a technical term meaning "homosexuals" (no such term existed in either Greek or Hebrew), but it appears as pejorative slang to describe the "passive" partners – often young boys – in homosexual activity. The other word, *arsenokoitai*, is not found in any extant Greek text earlier than 1 Corinthians. Some scholars have suggested that its meaning is uncertain, but Robin Scroggs has shown that the word is a translation of the Hebrew *mishkav zakur* ("lying with a male"), derived directly from Leviticus 18:22 and 20:13 and used in rabbinic texts to refer to homosexual intercourse. The Septuagint (Greek Old Testament) of Leviticus 20:13 reads, "Whoever lies with a man as with a woman [*meta arsenos koiten gynaikos*], they have done an abomination" (my translation). This is almost certainly the idiom from the noun *arsenokoitai* was coined. Thus, Paul's use of the term presupposes and reaffirms the holiness code's condemnation of homosexual acts.[280]

If Hays is right, then the terms employed in the NT passages are enough to include all homosexual activity and not just the kinds that Vines and Cannon would perceive as abusive.

Still, perhaps the strongest assertion for the Moral Permissive View is simply that no explicit rule prohibiting same-sex activity is ever given in the NT. However, to state the positive assertion of Biblical permissiveness on those grounds would be to postulate an argument from silence. This would be

---

[280] Richard Hays, *The Moral Vision of the New Testament* (San Francisco, CA: Harper One, 1996), 382.

the same (il)logical maneuver employed in perceiving Christian ethics as permissive of murder because there is not one direct prohibition of murder in the NT. The nearest to any such direct prohibition are the several references to Mosaic Law from Jesus and James, and it is worth noting that neither actually stated the mandate on its own merit outside of the Mosaic context. If homosexuality can be absolved this way, then so can murder.

While the aforementioned grounds for the Moral Permissive argument are persuasive to some, their limitations are not difficult to identify. Nonetheless, the emotional appeal and the simple peer pressure that results is perhaps the most persuasive of all. It is ironic, in the view of this writer, that kindness, compassion, and respect remain the most valuable influencers in favor of same-sex activity. Still, it is important to note that if these virtues are misplaced in advocating for homosexuality, then their persuasiveness is a mirage and even a deception. Kindness, compassion, and respect must be rooted in truth – just as the kind of love that drives orthopraxy is a particular kind of love – from a pure heart and a good conscience and a sincere faith.

MORAL PROHIBITIVE VIEW (LEGALITY THEOLOGY)

For the Roman Catholic thinker, the Moral Prohibitive View is a good fit. Historical tradition is clear about the moral illegality of homosexual activity: "Basing itself on Sacred Scripture, which presents acts of homosexuality as acts of grave depravity, tradition has always declared that 'homosexual acts are intrinsically disordered.' They are contrary to the natural law..."[281] Commendably, the *Catechism* calls those who might consider themselves homosexuals to chastity.[282] As the appeal to historical theology implies, there is a longstanding prohibition, about which, there has been little debate until more recently, as the RCC seeks to maintain cultural relevance. For the Reformed/Covenant thinker, the Moral Prohibitive View is the most natural fit, consistent with the theological hermeneutic that governs Reformed/Covenant understanding of the applicability of the Mosaic Law for the church today. In this view, because God legislates from His character, His legislation cannot change (as His character is immutable). Consequently, the Law *must* remain in effect.

Whereas advocates of the Moral Permissive View read the Bible through the lens of culture, proponents of the Moral Prohibitive View focus on several passages of Scripture through the lens of theology and tradition (or at least certain philosophical pre-commitments). While some of the several references are not definitive, it is the Mosaic legal references that are usually given the most weight in this approach.

Setting the context, and perhaps providing precedent, Genesis 19 records the judgment of Sodom, and while 19:5 records an attempted homosexual gang rape, homosexuality is not identified in the context as the reason for the impending judgment. In fact, it is obvious that the judgment was already on its way before the citizens of Sodom sought to commit that particular offense. Further, God Himself attributes the guilt of Sodom as "arrogance, abundant food and careless ease, but she did not help the poor and needy."[283] While He adds that also

---

[281] *Catholic Catechism*, Part 3, Section 2, Chapter 2, Article 6, 2357.
[282] Ibid., 2359.
[283] Ezekiel 16:49.

"they committed abominations,"[284] He does not specify the nature of those abominations. Jude 7 gets closer to directly addressing Sodom's homosexuality, citing "gross immorality" and going after strange flesh (*sarkos heteras*), but arguably the latter reference could be speaking of the angelic nature of the would-be victims. Still, Genesis 19 seems to set a clear precedent for the negativity of homosexual activity, but the passage is not definitive for that purpose.

Leviticus 18:22 and 20:13 contain the only clear Biblical prohibitions of or direct mandates against same-sex sexual activity. This context is part of the Law of Moses, and the Mosaic Covenant which was made with "the house of Jacob and the sons of Israel."[285] The question is whether or not mandates found within a conditional, targeted covenant are broadly applicable and ethically binding today. Advocates of the Moral Prohibitive View are generally clear that these mandates are binding. The essential premise here is that because the Law emanates from the character of God, the Law can't change, and is thus still in effect. This premise reads these legal passages through the lens of the theological conclusion regarding the nature of authority and God's immutability.

Greg Bahnsen, for example, speaks of the "abiding validity of the Law,"[286] suggesting the threefold division of the Law (moral, ceremonial, civil), and arguing that all three parts are equally binding, as evidenced by Matthew 5:17. Bahnsen holds to a strong Reformed/Covenant perspective that *authority is law*. God legislates from His character and can do no other.

---

[284] 16:50.

[285] Exodus 19:3.

[286] Greg Bahnsen, *Theonomy in Christian Ethics,* (Nacogdoches, TX: Covenant Media Press, 2002), ch. 2.

Because God's character is immutable, so must His law be also. Consequently, Christians today are under the Law, otherwise, God has violated His own character. Bahnsen's strong version of continuity[287] has been referred to as *theonomy*. He explains the applicability of the Law in a way consistent with his methodology: "The accomplishment of redemption changes the way in which we observe the ceremonial law, and the change of culture and times alters the specific ways in which we observe the case laws. The cases are different but the same moral principles remain."[288]

David Jones elucidates a semi-continuity[289] understanding that he recognizes as the prevailing sentiment of the church.[290] Because Acts 15 ruled the ceremonial law not applicable to NT believer, and because the NT voices approval of non-theocratic governments, thus rendering the civil law non applicable,[291] the believer is only under the moral law for sanctification.[292] Jones' version, like Bahnsen's is rooted in the idea that authority is law, but Jones' is a weaker or gentler version that allows for two of the three divisions of the Mosaic Law to have been fulfilled, with the immutability of God reflected in the unchanging moral law of the Ten Commandments: "Since the Decalogue is a reflection of God's

---

[287] My term to indicate that the Law continues to be in effect and broadly applicable.

[288] Greg Bahnsen, "The Faculty Discussion on Theonomy," Question 9, Reformed Theological Seminary, 1978, viewed at http://www.cmfnow.com/articles/pe192.htm.

[289] My term, to indicate that some of the Law continues and is applicable for today.

[290] David Jones, *Introduction to Biblical Ethics* (Nashville: TN, B&H Academic, 2013), 76.

[291] E.g., Romans 13:1-5, 1 Peter 2:13-17.

[292] Jones, 139.

moral character, the norms codified in the Ten Commandments are universally applicable and demonstrable both before and after their issuance on Mount Sinai."[293]

The implications of this commonly held Reformed/Covenant perspective of the Law are illustrated well by Samuel Bolton, who suggests that "The law sends us to the gospel that we may be justified, and the gospel sends us to the law again to enquire what is our duty in being justified."[294] Bolton's comments underscore the importance of the Law as the believer's moral duty. As the Gospel is applied, its impact is universal, as Jones notes, "As the kingdom of God grows, then the gospel gradually counteracts and corrects the effects of sin in the world through the process of restoration and reconciliation...the gospel is no less comprehensive than the fall..."[295] So both Bolton and Jones (along with the majority of Reformed/Covenant thinkers) recognize the broad societal responsibility and impact of the Gospel applied in sanctification, that is through obedience to the Decalogue. Yet, there are two significant flaws with this approach.

First, how can the threefold division of the Law be justified? That division is not a textual one, but rather a theological device. How can it be said that the other two alleged aspects of the Law (ceremonial and civil) do not have moral components and are not equally as binding? In fact, this inconsistency is evident when advocates of this understanding appeal to Leviticus 18 and 20 as a lasting basis for rejection of same-sex activity. If that section is part of the civil law, or even

---

[293] Ibid.
[294] Samuel Bolton, *True Bonds of Christian Freedom* (London, UK: Banner of Truth, 1964), 80.
[295] Jones, 64.

the ceremonial, then upon what basis can it be justified that these principles remain? This creates a dilemma for the "authority is law" argument. If God legislates from His character, then how can He cleanse what He once declared unclean? If He does so, then His legislation can change. If He does not, then stay away from pork, shellfish, and mixing cloths carelessly![296] Hays observes the problem:

> The Old Testament...makes no distinction between ritual law and moral law. The same section of the holiness code also contains, for instance, the prohibition of incest (Lev. 18:6-18). Is that a purity law or a moral law? Leviticus makes no distinction in principle. In each case, the church is tasked with discerning whether Israel's traditional norms remain in force for the new community of Jesus' followers. In order to see what decisions the early church made about this matter, we must turn to the New Testament.[297]

This begs the question that highlights the second significant flaw of the semi-continuity approach: Since James 2:10 tells us that if we stumble in one point we have violated all the Law, then how can any of these laws be changed without His express written or verbal direction? For example, notice how Jones handles the Sabbath, recognizing the tension between what was originally prescribed and what is the present habit of the church:

---

[296] E.g., Leviticus 11; Deuteronomy 22:11.
[297] Richard Hays, *The Moral Vision of the New Testament:* (San Francisco, CA: Harper One, 1996), 382.

For Christians, then, the Sabbath is a sign of redemption and, as such, it depicts the eternal rest they have received from Jesus in salvation...Keeping the Sabbath ought not to be a legalistic burden, characterized by lists of permitted and forbidden activities. Rather the Sabbath ought to be a joyous celebration and a blessing...In a specific sense the fourth commandment calls believers to observe a regular day of worship...not to observe the Sabbath, in either a broad or a specific sense, is to behave in a distinctly un-Christlike manner...in the NT...the early church moved the day of Sabbath observance to the first day of the week.[298]

The problems created by this statement are several. First, Jones characterizes without exegetical warrant the Sabbath as a sign of redemption for Christians, when it is expressly a sign between God and Israel.[299] Who determines the meaning of the sign if there is no textual data?[300]   Second, he suggests the sabbath shouldn't be a legalistic burden, but the fourth commandment *was* a legal burden; he argues that it shouldn't be characterized by lists of permitted and forbidden activities, but in fact, that is exactly what the Sabbath was – and there are actually lists of

---

[298] Jones, 166.

[299] Exodus 20:12.

[300] Hebrews 4 makes use of the Sabbath to illustrate a future reality for believers, but it does not at all invalidate the literal nature of the Sabbath, nor the carefully described sign component of the Sabbath for Israel (Ex 20:12, etc.), nor of the ethical requirement of the Sabbath within the Mosaic Law. Further, if the Law (even simply the moral aspect) is applicable for believers today, then the literal aspect must be upheld, regardless of any metaphorical application of the Sabbath concept.

forbidden activities.[301] Third, he suggests that the commandment is a call to observe a regular day of worship, when the text demands that it be a day of rest. Finally, he suggests that the church moved the day of Sabbath observance. Based on what authority could the church have done that, and where in Scripture do we see that actually happen? The semi-continuity view of the Law is problematic in light of James 2:10, and without some direct prescription, if the church moved the Sabbath then the church is guilty in the James 2:10 sense.

Now, if the Law was given to Israel only, has not been divided, but has been fulfilled in whole, then the two Leviticus passages cannot be seen as presently applicable prohibitions against homosexuality. If on the other hand, the Law has been given more broadly than simply to Israel, and has been divided, and has not been completely fulfilled, then ironically Christ ultimately has little if anything to do with Christian ethics, as His church is simply bound by Mosaic Law. And in the authority is law model, Christ couldn't change or fulfill the Law if He wanted to, lest He find Himself at odds with the character of His Father.

Besides the sticky conundrum of the applicability of the Law, there is another problem for the Moral Prohibitive View – outside of the Leviticus passages, there are simply no direct prohibitions of homosexual activity. Kevin DeYoung, recognizing the challenges such an absence creates, crafts his argument on a cumulative case:

> There is nothing in the biblical text to suggest Paul or Moses or anyone else meant to limit the Scriptural

---

301 Exodus 20:10, 35:2-3.

condemnation of homosexual behavior. Likewise, there is no good reason to think from the thousands of homosexuality-related texts found in the Greco-Roman period that the blanket rejection of homosexual behavior found in the Bible can be redeemed by postulating an impassable cultural distance between our world and the ancient world. There is simply no positive case for homosexual practice in the Bible and no historical background that will allow us to set aside what has been the plain reading of Scripture for twenty centuries.[302]

While what DeYoung says here is not incorrect, it is – like the strongest argument for the Moral Permissive approach – an argument from silence. Essentially, DeYoung asserts that since the tone of Scripture is negative toward homosexuality, there is no positive case to be made favoring homosexuality. So far so good. But the implied conclusion is that there is a present day, practical prohibition in place. This argument from silence is better than that of the Moral Permissive View, because Moral Permissive has the arduous task of shedding the weight of Scripture's negativity toward homosexuality, while at least the Moral Prohibitive View lands on the correct side of the data. Still, DeYoung's argument is limited in that it does not provide certainty regarding what is the authentic Christian ethic for today. While both views suffer from the argument from silence as their *coup de gras*, the third view does not share that particular limitation.

---

[302] Kevin DeYoung, "Not That Kind of Homosexuality," The Gospel Coalition, November 13, 2014, viewed at https://www.thegospelcoalition.org/blogs/kevin-deyoung/not-that-kind-of-homosexuality/.

INHERENT DESIGN VIEW (DESIGN THEOLOGY)

When we read culture through the lens of the Bible, rather than the Bible through the lens of culture, we often find clarity. Genesis 19 (when coupled with Jude 7) and Leviticus 18:22 and 20:13 are all strongly negative toward same-sex activity. With forcefulness the Mosaic Law prohibits homosexual activity, however, in a literal grammatical historical handling of Scriptures pertaining to the Mosaic Law, we must conclude that this was a conditional covenant exclusively for Israel, and that it was completely fulfilled in Christ, and now it serves the purpose as a tutor leading people to Christ.[303] The Christian is not under the Mosaic Law in any way – not for justification, and not for sanctification. Further, the Mosaic Law is not ethically applicable to the church beyond the purpose spelled out expressly in Scripture.

Consequently, it is evident that God *can* change (or fulfill) His legislation, and His use of that ability creates no friction for the literal grammatical historical understanding, as God is clearly presented as Sovereign over all His creation. Thus, His authority is over law – law does not emanate from His character, it emanates from Him, when He chooses to give it. In this understanding there is no theological need for the threefold division of the Law, and since there is no exegetical warrant for inferring such a division, this approach is not guilty of eisegesis in this regard. Further, there is only one ethical standard for the Christian, and it is not the Mosaic Law (though it is referenced in that Law[304]), it is the holiness of God.[305] In light of God's

---

[303] Galatians 3:24-25.
[304] E.g., Leviticus 11:45, 19:2, 20:7, 20:26, etc.
[305] 1 Peter 1:15.

holiness there are two distinct sets of ethical applications – one set for unbelievers (respect the sanctity of life[306] and believe in Christ[307]), and one set for believers (essentially, be holy). Unbelievers are not called to live holy lives according God's design – they are called to believe in their Creator, and then to walk in holiness. This concept helps us understand how 1 Corinthians 6:9 and 1 Timothy 1:10 are vitally connected to the design issue.

In 1 Corinthians 6:9 and 1 Timothy 1:10 are found characterizations that *arsenokoitai* are unrighteous and contrary to sound teaching, and as such, will not inherit the kingdom of God. The solution is also identified in 1 Corinthians 6:10 – be washed, sanctified, justified. Neither passage is teaching that homosexuality (or any other sin) is unforgiveable, on the contrary, some of the Corinthian believers were involved in exactly that, and yet they were redeemed. The implication is *not* that if one engages in any of these acts they will lose access to the Kingdom, rather the characterization is of the unrighteous (by nature) who express their unrighteousness in these particular symptomatic ways. The challenge in both of these passages is for believers not to live in the contrary absurdity as if they are positionally and by nature unrighteous, doing the deeds of unrighteousness – why should one who is redeemed and empowered by the Holy Spirit live like someone who will not inherit the Kingdom? That would be as illogical as *not* presenting our bodies a living and holy sacrifice – because *that* is our logical service of worship.

---

[306] Genesis 9.
[307] Genesis 15:6, Habakkuk 2:4, John 20:30-31.

Both of these passages are clear enough in describing homosexuality (along with lists of other activities) as displeasing to God. And if all we had were Genesis 19, Leviticus 18:22, 20:13, 1 Corinthians 6:9, and 1 Timothy 1:10, those passages alone would provide an incredible weight of clarity regarding the wrongness of homosexual activity. But when we examine the teleological component that God reveals in Scripture, especially in light of the culminating pericope of Romans 1, we can draw no other conclusion than homosexuality is a violation of God's created order,[308] and *that is why it is presented so negatively in the other passages.*

Six Teleological Elements

As we consider God's design for humanity, six aspects are evident. First is the *Design Question* – In Genesis 1:27 we read that God created man in His own image, in the image of God He created him; male (*zaqar*) and female (*negebah*) He created them. *But why did He create two sexes, male and female?* He could have done anything He wished, and yet it was His plan to create male and female. The simple answer is that there is no answer given in Scripture, so we leave it to the Designer to maintain His trade secrets. He has the authority to have chosen the design He did.

Second, we consider the *Design Deficiency.* God built into His creation an inherent deficiency. The first time in history we see anything referred to as not good, it is God's observation of Adam's aloneness. Adam did not have a helper (an opposite) corresponding to him.[309] It is worth noting that the male sex

---

[308] Going far beyond Aquinas' and the RCC's appeal to natural law.
[309] Genesis 2:18.

already existed. Why didn't God just create another one of the same kind so that Adam would have companionship? Part of the answer may be seen in God's parading the animals before Adam so Adam could recognize how they were designed – male and female as counterpart, for procreation and other apparent reasons. Surely Adam would have also noticed the physical differences in the way the two sexes were built beyond their sexual capacities. Their anatomies were *designed* differently. The two would fulfill different roles and purposes, far beyond simply procreation. By contrast, Adam was at that point unique in that he had no counterpart.

Third, we see the *Design Resolution* in Genesis 2:18b-24. God said "I will make him a helper suitable for him."[310] That helper (*ezer*) was a woman. She was corresponding to or opposite (*neged*) him. Notice the prescriptive element in 2:24 – "For this reason a man shall leave his father and his mother and be joined to his wife; and they shall become one flesh." The proper expression of the design for togetherness is accomplished in marriage. It is stated simply and rooted in the created order.

Fourth, we encounter the *Design Affirmation*, as Jesus affirms the veracity and foundational nature of the creation story and how God Himself has joined man and woman.[311] Jesus affirmed the design in the created order, and affirmed monogamous, heterosexual marriage based on that design. If that is the design, then what of those who are not married? Are they in violation of that design? Are they dysfunctional in some way?

---

[310] Genesis 2:18b.
[311] Matthew 19:4-6.

Paul addresses that question in the fifth point, providing the *Design Alternative*. In 1 Corinthians 7:8 and 17 Paul extols the high value of celibacy. Humanity is designed for marriage, but some are gifted, even called for celibacy. There are few giftings and callings actually spelled out in Scripture. It is rather remarkable that being single is referenced by both terms. The *designed* alternative for the *design* of marriage is to remain single or celibate – these are the two provided and positively stated paths for proper expression of sexuality.

One might ask at this point whether or not God has called or gifted any to homosexuality. If the design includes one positively stated alternative, then is it possible there is a second alternative? This is where the Inherent Design View avoids the argument from silence and instead argues from revelation that the single and exclusive alternative to the original design is revealed quantifiably in 1 Corinthians 7. Is it possible there is a second alternative? No, because the alternative is based on God's gifting and calling, and *to be certain* of God's gifting and calling in this context requires that He has revealed that there is such a gifting and calling. How can one walk in a supposed calling or gifting if they have no evidence that calling or gifting has come from Him? On what basis could they claim it is a calling or gifting at all? On the other hand, if one is married, they have that gifting and calling. If one is single/celibate they have that gifting and calling. If one is engaging in homosexual activity, that is defined neither as gift nor calling, but is, in every single instance in Scripture, presented as contrary to the design, not as a legitimate alternative.

That contrary activity is the sixth component: *Design Abandonment*. In Romans 1:18-20 is described how the truth of God is suppressed in unrighteousness. Verses 21-23 explains how a rejection of the Designer results in an obvious rejection of the design. Verses 24-25 identify consequence #1 – the unrighteous are given over to desires – allowed to pursue their own alternatives, since they have rejected their Creator and His design and the inherent alternative (celibacy) within His design. Verses 26-27 identify consequence #2 – the unrighteous are given over to that which is unnatural. They are allowed to take things to their logical conclusion. The Designer and the design are utterly rejected, and all that is left is the pursuit of the unnatural (that which violates the design) and the final consequence (#3) listed in 1:28 – they are given over to brokenness of mind. While God has gifted, assigned, and called humanity with marriage and some individuals with celibacy, those that have rejected Him and His design He has given over to pursue their own design along with all the associated brokenness that comes with that pursuit.

As a culminating discussion of God's design for humanity, it is obvious that there are no alternatives besides heterosexual marriage or celibacy commended or prescribed – and those two options are explicitly prescribed. Further it is evident that the homosexual "option" is presented in context not as a legitimate alternative, but as a total distortion of what God designed. Romans 1 completes the teleological cumulative case that provides certainty in Christian ethics regarding same-sex activity. To insure that none us can boast or condemn from a perch of innocence, the context of 1:29-2:2 reiterates that we all are universally guilty, and that we have all committed acts against God that render us worthy of death. All of us like sheep have gone astray, each to his own way, but the Lord has caused the iniquity of us all to fall upon Him.[312]

While the Inherent Design View overcomes the limitations of the other two views, namely in that it (1) is more methodologically consistent with a literal grammatical historical approach to the Scriptures, (2) draws exegetically justifiable conclusions about the character of God and the origin of morality, and (3) recognizes the progress of revelation allowing for both a cogency and discontinuity in God's revelation on the matter, there is an additional element that this writer finds compelling. This is not a device for justifying or condemning a particular lifestyle, rather it is an attempt at simply understanding what and who our Creator has designed us to be, and how we can be restored to right relationship with Him when we fail to walk as designed. God isn't a hateful Creator who has excluded those who identify as LGBTQ from intimacy and joy. On the contrary, He has put in place a design wherein we can all experience the richest of His blessings through His grace as we come to know Him and the pattern He gave to us, so that we might see His fingerprints in our lives, submit to Him as our Designer, and rejoice. It is when we encounter the profound nature of our Designer, as revealed in His design, that we can respond as prescribed with the right kind of love toward Him and toward others – love from a pure heart, a good conscience, and a sincere faith.

---

[312] Isaiah 53:6.

CHAPTER 8

EVERY TRIBE, TONGUE, PEOPLE, AND NATION: THE FUTURE OF RACE RELATIONS AND SOCIAL JUSTICE IMPLICATIONS FOR TODAY[313]

"But the one who hates his brother is in the darkness and walks in the darkness, and does not know where he is going because the darkness has blinded his eyes."[314]

INTRODUCTION

Jesus' presentation of the kingdom of the heavens in Matthew 5-7 was particularly intended for first-century Jewish people to understand that internal righteousness and not simply external adherence to moral code was necessary to enter that kingdom. In addition to demonstrating this key deficiency on the part of His listeners, His Sermon on the Mount further offers a model for the character of kingdom members and the culture of the kingdom, and thus has contemporary applications, since

---

[313] Presented to the Council on Dispensational Hermeneutics at Calvary University, Kansas City, Missouri, September 19, 2019.
[314] *New American Standard Bible: 1995 Update* (La Habra, CA: The Lockman Foundation, 1995), 1 Jn 2:11.

believers in Jesus during the church age have been transferred (positionally) to His kingdom.[315] While that kingdom currently has no (other) earthly expression in this age, it will one day come to earth in literal fulfillment of God's kingdom promises in physical manifestation (hence, Matthew's term "kingdom of the heavens"), thus the applicability of the Sermon for the present day is strengthened by the future certainty of kingdom-promise fulfillment. If it is appropriate to understand the Sermon on the Mount as having contemporary implications for character and ethics in general (because of the kingdom citizenship component of church-age believers), then future aspects of the kingdom and of the two intertwining destinies (heavenly and earthly) show a model of God's design for the future of human relations.

This study (a) introduces several ideological diagnoses of social injustice with their respective prescriptions, (b) illustrates the extent of the problem as expressed in racial disunity, (c) outlines the solution expressed in Biblical eschatology, and (d) examines the hermeneutic legitimacy of contemporary application of the Sermon on the Mount, and of its future aspects and the destinies implied for its citizens, especially in light of the "every tribe" inclusiveness found in passages like Genesis 12:3b, Revelation 5:9, 7:9, 10:11, 11:9, 13:7, 14:6, 16:10, and 17:15. The resulting focus on human relationships and ethnic diversity in the kingdom helps us consider the implications of that diversity for the present-day church and its interactions with society, particularly on the topics of race and unity, with a view to candid and robust dialogue as we together pursue God's design for His church.

---

[315] Colossians 1:13.

THREE IDEOLOGICAL MODELS FOR SOCIAL JUSTICE

An oft-repeated description of social justice suggests that it "entails a 'redistribution' of resources from those who have "unjustly" gained them to those who justly deserve them..."[316] Some might accept a less specific attribution, that "[s]ocial justice is really the capacity to organize with others to accomplish ends that benefit the whole community."[317] Still, in popular usage the term seems to most generally imply, "among other things, equality of the burdens, the advantages, and the opportunities of citizenship...social justice is intimately related to the concept of equality, and that the violation of it is intimately related to the concept of inequality."[318]

Model 1 – An Ecclesiastical Approach:
The Amillennial Economic Mean Between Individualism and Collectivism

Probably first coined by Jesuit philosopher Luigi Taparelli d'Azeglio in 1843,[319] the term *social justice* for him represented the "constitutional justice of a society, the justice

---

[316] Joe R. Feagin, "Social Justice and Sociology: Agendas for the Twenty-First Century" in *Critical Strategies for Social Research* ed. William K. Carroll (Toronto: Canadian Scholars' Press, 2004), 32.

[317] Michael Novak, "Social Justice: Not What You Think It Is" *The Heritage Foundation*, December 29, 2009, viewed at: https://www.heritage.org/poverty-and-inequality/report/social-justice-not-what-you-think-it.

[318] G. J. Papageorgiou, "Social Values and Social Justice," *Economic Geography*, Vol. 56, No. 2 (April 1980), pp. 110-119.

[319] Thomas Patrick Burke, "The Origins of Social Justice: Taparelli d'Azeglio" in *Modern Age*, Spring 2019: 98, referring to by Luigi Taparelli d'Azeglio in Saggio teoretico di dritto naturale appoggiato sul fatto, 5 vols. (Palermo, 1843).

that defends right order in the constitutional arrangements of the society. Its task at that juncture of history, he believed, was to defend the inherited rights of the existing powers, the Church and the aristocracy, against the rising tide of democratic equality."[320] Taparelli opposed the capitalism of John Locke and Adam Smith because "he saw liberalism as a product of the Protestant Reformation, which exalted private judgment over the divine authority of the Roman Catholic Church and thereby replaced the Catholic sense of community with an emphasis on the self-interest of the isolated individual."[321] Still, Taparelli's was not an economic core.

Though building on Taparelli's foundation, Pope Pius XI focused almost exclusively on the economic aspects of social justice, a term which soon came to represent "a new kind of virtue (or habit) necessary for post-agrarian societies…"[322] From within this anti-individualistic stream of economic theory, Pius XI's 1931 encyclical *Quadragesimo Anno*[323] epitomized the social justice mandate for the Roman Catholic Church. The encyclical sought to address "that difficult problem of human relations called 'the social question,'"[324] and along with Leo XIII's 1891 encyclical, *On the Condition of Workers,* proposed "a true Catholic social science."[325] Quoting Leo XIII, Pius XI reaffirms that, the Church "strives not only to instruct the mind, but to regulate by her precepts the life and morals of individuals, and

---

[320] Ibid.: 105.

[321] Ibid.: 104.

[322] Novak, Ibid.

[323] Penned by Oswald von Nell-Bruening S.J..

[324] Pope Pius XI "*Quadragisimo Anno*" 1931, 2, viewed at: http://w2.vatican.va/content/pius-xi/en/encyclicals/documents/hf_p-xi_enc_19310515_quadragesimo-anno.html.

[325] Ibid., 20.

that ameliorates the condition of the workers through her numerous and beneficent institutions."[326]

Pius XI combats the "twin rocks of shipwreck,"[327] namely *individualism*, which he suggests is fostered when the social and collective aspects of property ownership are ignored, and *collectivism*, on the other hand, which thrives when personal property rights are minimized. To strike the necessary balance, he reminds the reader that, "there resides in Us the right and duty to pronounce with supreme authority upon social and economic matters."[328] In this Pius XI distinguishes the Catholic doctrine of social justice from its secular counterpart (socialism): because "man is older than the State,"[329] the state doesn't have the right to define or infringe upon property rights. Rather those authorities reside with the Church. Pius XI emphasizes that, "the deposit of truth that God committed to Us and the grave duty of disseminating and interpreting the whole moral law, and of urging it in season and out of season, *bring under and subject to Our supreme jurisdiction not only social order but economic activities themselves* [emphasis mine]."[330] The Church, by virtue of the cultural mandate, has jurisdiction beyond that of the state.

Pius XI asserted that not only was the state insufficient for handling such challenges, the free market also lacked the capacity to properly regulate society, as he made clear in stating that "right ordering of economic life cannot be left to a free competition of forces. For from this source, as from a poisoned

---

[326] Ibid., 17.
[327] Ibid., 46.
[328] Ibid., 41.
[329] Ibid., 49.
[330] Ibid., 41.

spring, have originated and spread all the errors of individualist economic teaching."[331] On the basis of natural law, then, neither the state, nor an entirely free market were fitted to govern society, but only the Church had divinely appropriated access and the mandate to provide the hermeneutic underpinnings necessary for the proper economic ordering of society." Christian social philosophy, must be kept in mind regarding ownership and labor and their association together, and must be put into actual practice."[332]

This practice and right ordering avoid the two great errors of individualism and the capitalism that fosters it, and collectivism and the brand of socialism leading to communism that solidifies it. Pius XI prescribes a kinder gentler sort of socialism that "inclines toward and in a certain measure approaches the truths which Christian tradition has always held sacred"[333] But he is careful not to prescribe socialism in its pure sense, warning that, "Socialism, if it remains truly Socialism, even after it has yielded to truth and justice on the points which we have mentioned, cannot be reconciled with the teachings of the Catholic Church because its concept of society itself is utterly foreign to Christian truth.[334] Specifically, the deficiency is evident in that socialism "affirms that human association has been instituted for the sake of material advantage alone,"[335] consequently, Pius XI concludes that "no one can be at the same time a good Catholic and a true socialist,"[336] and exhorts readers

---

[331] Ibid., 88.
[332] Ibid., 110.
[333] Ibid., 113.
[334] Ibid., 117.
[335] Ibid., 118.
[336] Ibid., 120.

not to "permit the children of this world to appear wiser in their generation than we who by the Divine Goodness are the children of the light."[337] The solution for inequality and oppression is to be found not in either economic system of capitalism nor socialism/communism, but in Christian truth as disseminated and interpreted by the Catholic Church.

Model 2 – The Statist Approach:
Collectivist Abolition of Free Trade as the Economic Messiah

In the Preface to the 1888 English edition of *The Manifesto of the Communist Party*, Frederick Engels introduces the fundamental proposition of communism as follows:

> That in every historical epoch, the prevailing mode of economic production and exchange, and the social organization necessarily following from it, form the basis upon which it is built up, and from that which alone can be explained the political and intellectual history of that epoch; that consequently the whole history of mankind (since the dissolution of primitive tribal society, holding land in common ownership) has been a history of class struggles, contests between exploiting and exploited, ruling and oppressed classes; That the history of these class struggles forms a series of evolutions in which, nowadays, a stage has been reached where the exploited and oppressed class – the proletariat – cannot attain its emancipation from the sway of the exploiting and ruling class – the bourgeoisie – without, at the same time, and once and for all, emancipating society at large from all

---

[337] Ibid., 146.

exploitation, oppression, class distinction, and class struggles.[338]

For Marx and Engels social justice (even though they don't use the term in the document, as it hadn't yet come into vogue) hinged on resolving class struggle, which meant reforming the economic engines of inequality, primarily, by eliminating distinctions through the implemented communist ideal. While socialism was not philosophically dissimilar from Marx' and Engels' communism, they viewed socialism as a middle-class enterprise and communism as a working-class effort. Thus, communism would be more efficacious in actually bringing about change.[339]

Economics, and capitalism specifically, is asserted to be a catalyst for destructive societal forces. Marx and Engels posit a better economic model as the solution. Karl Polanyi asserted that "To allow the market mechanism to be sole director of the fate of human beings and the natural environment, indeed, even of the amount and use of purchasing power, would result in the demolition of society."[340] Feagin expresses four significant deficiencies in capitalist economies and societies.[341] Problem #1: Capitalism transfers wealth from the poor and working classes to the rich and affluent social classes: "in most countries great income and wealth inequalities create major related injustices, including shar differentials in hunger, housing, life satisfaction,

---

[338] Karl Marx and Frederick Engels, Preface to the 1888 English Edition, *Manifesto of the Communist Party*, (From *Marx/Engels Selected Works, Vol. One*, Progress Publishers, Moscow, 1969, 98-137), 8.
[339] Ibid.
[340] Feagin, 29.
[341] Ibid., 30-32.

life expectancy, and political power."[342] Problem #2: Capitalism (through the exploitation of transnational corporations) brings disruption and marginalization to many. Problem #3: Capitalism takes a heavy toll on the environment. Problem #4: Capitalism fosters racial and ethnic inequality and oppression, homophobia, and other inequities. Racial divides are perceived as an economic problem, with economic solutions as the cure.

The specific problem diagnosed in the *Manifesto* is the systematic bourgeoisie abuse of the working class (proletariat) in "shameless, direct, brutal exploitation"[343] primarily through the "single unconscionable freedom – Free Trade."[344] Only the proletariat has the capability to end the ongoing economic cycle through revolution. The other classes – like the lower middle class – "decay and finally disappear in the face of Modern Industry."[345] Marx and Engels viewed the lower middle class not as revolutionary enough to bring lasting change, but rather motivated in their own fight against the bourgeoisie, "to save from extinction their existence as fractions of the middle class. They are therefore not revolutionary, but conservative... reactionary, for they try to roll back the wheel of history."[346] Only the proletariat has the capacity for effective revolution, for it is their labor that has been commodified as the capital which greases the economic wheels of a free market that benefits the bourgeoisie to the detriment of all else. As Marx and Engels seek to inspire the working class to revolution and a new economic model (communism), they prophecy that, "the bourgeoisie

---

[342] Ibid., 30.
[343] Marx and Engels., 16.
[344] Ibid.
[345] Ibid., 20.
[346] Ibid.

therefore produces, above all, are its own grave-diggers. Its fall and the victory of the proletariat are equally inevitable."[347]

One critical means for the resolution of class struggle is the abolition of private property, for communism "deprives no man of the power to appropriate the products of society; all that it does is to deprive him of the power to subjugate the labour of others by means of such appropriations."[348] In short, if anyone can own property it will be the bourgeoisie, and the bourgeoisie have always oppressed the proletariat by capitalizing the labor of the proletariat in order to get property. Since the proletariat rarely ever get property anyway, if there is no ownership of property at all, then the bourgeoisie can't oppress the proletariat, and the proletariat haven't lost anything, plus then they would be free from oppression.

Beyond the abolition of property, Marx and Engels want to abolish the family by replacing "home education with social."[349] The refined educational model "seek[s] to alter the character of that intervention, and to rescue education from the influence of the ruling class."[350] Ultimately, this protects proletariat children from being "transformed into simple articles of commerce and instruments of labour."[351] Further developments of communism include the abolition of national differences and nationalism (in favor of the partisanship of communism),[352] in seeking to eliminate oppression of the ruling class through ideas, religion is abolished – "The Communist

---

[347] Ibid., 21.
[348] Ibid., 24.
[349] Ibid.
[350] Ibid.
[351] Ibid., 25.
[352] Ibid.

revolution is the most radical rupture with traditional property relations; no wonder that its development involved the most radical rupture with traditional ideas."[353] Eternal truths, religion, and morality are traded in as part of traditional, patriarchal, ruling class societal norms that must be removed if there is to be revolution suitable for installing lasting equality. Thus, if the working class unite (in the communist ideal), as prescribed, then "In place of the old bourgeois society, with its classes and class antagonisms, we shall have an association, in which the free development of each is the condition for the free development of all."[354]

Marx' and Engels' prescription of communism as the economic remedy for inequality and oppression demands that the state set boundaries and ultimately manage the ownership of property, effectually eliminating individualism. The Catholic response to that concept, from Leo XIII and Pius XI, is the assertion that the state could claim no right to take such sweeping oversight. Both the secular and the ecclesiastical, however, agreed that individualism was not a viable solution, and was in fact a common enemy. These two models – Marx' and Engels' secular and the Catholic non-secular models, while sharing a mutual distaste for individualism, are rooted in competing views of human nature and of authority itself, have pursued, to date, mutually exclusive political power in order to exact the kinds of societal evolution necessary to achieve their respective ends. The paths to social justice for these two models scarcely intersect, but they are remarkably intertwined in iterations of Liberation Theology.

---

[353] Ibid., 26.
[354] Ibid., 27.

Model 3 – The Liberation Theology Synthesis: Postmillennial Dominionism

Gustavo Gutiérrez is credited with originating the term Liberation Theology, in his 1971 publication, *Teología de la liberación*. Gutiérrez defines theology as "a critical reflection on the Church's presence and activity in the world, in the light of revelation,"[355] adding that "Theology is reflection, a critical attitude. First comes the commitment to charity, to service. Theology comes "later." It is second. *The Church's pastoral action is not arrived at as a conclusion from theological premises*. Theology does not lead to pastoral activity but is rather a reflection on it. [emphasis mine]"[356] For Gutiérrez, theology is not the product of exegetical analysis, but rather is much more broadly construed – this is in part reflects a logical expression of the Catholic hermeneutic of interpreting the Bible according to the tradition of the Church.[357] Theology is active, and a "variable understanding,"[358] addressing the needs of the moment.

In Gutiérrez' estimation liberation has three components: "the political liberation of oppressed peoples and social classes; man's liberation in the course of history; and liberation from sin as condition of a life of communion of all men with the Lord."[359] The mandate for liberation of the oppressed is rooted in a theological extrapolation of redemption by way of the Catholic

---

[355] Gustavo Gutiérrez, "Notes For a Theology of Liberation" in Theological Studies (Lima, Peru), 244. Viewed at http://cdn.theologicalstudies.net/31/31.2/31.2.1.pdf.
[356] Ibid., 244-245.
[357] *Catechism of the Catholic Church*, 113. Viewed at http://www.vatican.va/archive/ccc_css/archive/catechism/p1s1c2a3.htm.
[358] Gutiérrez, 244.
[359] Ibid., 248.

Church-tradition hermeneutic. The "redemptive work embraces every dimension of human existence."[360] Consequently, liberation becomes *part* of theology, with an "eschatological hope"[361] of social revolution.

The dominionist premise provides the means for achieving that eschatological hope, as Gutiérrez posits, "Mastering the earth, as Genesis bids him do, is a work of salvation, meant to produce its plenitude. To work, to transform this world, is to save...it means participating fully in the salvific process that affects the whole man."[362] Not only is Christ "the Saviour who, by liberating us from sin, liberates us from the very root of social injustice,"[363] but humanity, by way of the dominion mandate is co-participant in that salvific enterprise.

Inadequacy of the Three Models

Tracing these three streams through the lenses of Leo XIII and Pius XI, Marx and Engels, and Gutiérrez certainly constitutes no comprehensive analysis of the history of social justice (that would be far beyond the scope of this present work), but merely an *introduction of context for opposing foundations* of social justice in the contemporary western mind. Further, this context-setting provides the helpful backdrop for the consideration of contemporary application of the Sermon on the Mount – a central theme of this project.

Still, these streams and their advocates were focused on equality in relation to economic underpinnings as governed either by the church, the state, or some combination of both. But

---

[360] Ibid., 255.
[361] Ibid., 253.
[362] Ibid., 256.
[363] Ibid., 257.

each of these streams to date have proved deficient in their economic and political prescriptions, as they have not sufficiently addressed the root cause of the symptoms. Each of the three models diagnosed symptoms and prescribed solutions. The RCC asserted the faults of the extremes of individualism and collectivism, and prescribed an Aristotelian golden economic mean insured by the church. Marxism asserted the evils of class struggle resulting from free trade and sought a statist economic control to extinguish any hint of oppression-inciting free trade. Liberation theology pinpointed the problem as failing to fulfill the dominion mandate and synthesized the RCC and Marxist prescriptions to seek a church-driven political revolution that would complete the liberation of the whole man. To this point, while encountering varying degrees of success, each of these prescriptions has failed to accomplish its stated goal, at least in part because the problems diagnosed were symptomatic and not causative. The root cause of injustice and oppression is neither economic nor political, but rather was rooted simply *in the devaluation of human life that naturally results from the spiritually bankrupt devaluing of the Creator.* With good reason Solomon asserted that "the fear of the Lord is the beginning of wisdom, and the knowledge of the Holy One is understanding."[364]

The Biblical record inextricably links the proper valuation of human life to the right perspective of and response to the Creator. Genesis 1:26-27 sets the linkage as the created origin of humanity and the image of God in humanity. Genesis 9:5-6 underscores the sacredness of human life based on that linkage. Romans 5:12 asserts the universal need and traces it

---

[364] Proverbs 9:10.

back to Adam's sin and the hereditary consequence for all of subsequent humanity, while 5:18 describes how God likewise provided for the resolution of that problem for all of humanity. John 3:16 and 12:32 explain how God has reached out to all humanity. God's intention of delivering all of humanity is expressed in 1 Timothy 2:4, and the universal accessibility to that deliverance is pronounced in Titus 2:11. Because of the love of God expressed and executed through His redemptive plan, we have a new ontological unity in Christ, explained in Ephesians 2:14-18. Consequently, as Galatians 6:10 expresses, believers are to prioritize brothers and sisters in Christ, and *to do good to all*. That same love that God demonstrated for His created beings, we are to show toward one another, as Philippians 2:1-11 indicates. Humanity is created in God's image, valued based on God's image in us, saved because of God's grace, and expected to do good to one another as expressive and illustrative of His grace. Titus 3:1-7 lays out an application of this progression of thought: there is (1) an ethical expectation (including showing consideration for all humanity), (2) because once we were in need, (3) and because of God's love for all, (4) He saved us through Jesus Christ, (5) making us heirs of eternal life, (6) thus, there is an expectation based on our relationship to Him, and (7) because it is good for others:

> 1 Remind them to be subject to rulers, to authorities, to be obedient, to be ready for every good deed, 2 to malign no one, to be peaceable, gentle, showing every consideration for all men. 3 For we also once were foolish ourselves, disobedient, deceived, enslaved to various lusts and pleasures, spending our life in malice and envy, hateful, hating one another. 4 But when the kindness of

God our Savior and *His* love for mankind appeared, 5 He saved us, not on the basis of deeds which we have done in righteousness, but according to His mercy, by the washing of regeneration and renewing by the Holy Spirit, 6 whom He poured out upon us richly through Jesus Christ our Savior, 7 so that being justified by His grace we would be made heirs according to *the* hope of eternal life. 8 This is a trustworthy statement; and concerning these things I want you to speak confidently, so that those who have believed God will be careful to engage in good deeds. These things are good and profitable for men.[365]

These passages are emblematic of the univocal Biblical perspective that proper valuation of human life is rooted in proper valuation of the Creator, and that proper expression of that valuation in action cannot be unlinked from the epistemological premise that God has the right as the Creator to define reality and valuation itself – and that He has done so. Nor can orthodox expression of valuation in practice be unlinked from the metaphysical realities that God has revealed in Scripture. As John succinctly puts it, "If someone says, "I love God," and hates his brother, he is a liar; for the one who does not love his brother whom he has seen, cannot love God whom he has not seen."[366] *Position undergirds practice, and where there is faulty practice, there is neglect of positional truths.*

---

[365] Titus 3:1–8.
[366] 1 John 4:20.

A CASE STUDY IN FAILURE: POST-CIVIL WAR AMERICA AND THE FREEDMEN'S BUREAU

For any who might opine that there is no contemporary need for resolution of events more than a century past, W.E.B. Dubois' observations help to clarify the heartbreaking prominence of the "color line" especially immediately following the Civil War. Dubois characterizes the era as representative of an ever-unasked question, "How does it feel to be a problem?"[367] Dubois recognizes that during and from this time there was external perspective by those outside the black community that there was a problem to be resolved. Likewise, and perhaps consequently, there was internal perspective of individuals within the community that there was indeed a problem, and that problem, according to Dubois would create a painful rift for these men and women: "The history of the American Negro is the history of this strife – this longing to attain self-conscious manhood, to merge his double self into a better and truer self. In this merging he wishes neither of the older selves to be lost. He would not Africanize America, for America has too much to teach the world and Africa. He would not bleach his Negro soul in a flood of white Americanism, for he knows that Negro blood has a message for the world. He simply wishes to make it possible for a man to be both a Negro and an American, without being cursed and spit upon by his fellows, without having the doors of Opportunity closed roughly in his face."[368] "This, then, is the end of his striving: to be a co-worker in the kingdom of culture, to

---

[367] W.E.B. Dubois, *The Souls of Black Folk* (Oxford, UK: Oxford University Press, 2007), 7.
[368] Dubois, 9.

escape both death and isolation, to husband and use his best powers and his latent genius.[369]

Dubois understood this duality of oppositional cultures to create an unworkable situation in practice: "The double-aimed struggle of the black artisan—on the one hand to escape white contempt for a nation of mere hewers of wood and drawers of water, and on the other hand to plough and nail and dig for a poverty-stricken horde— could only result in making him a poor craftsman, for he had but half a heart in either cause... this seeking to satisfy two unreconciled ideals, has wrought sad havoc with the courage and faith and deeds of ten thousand thousand people,—has sent them often wooing false gods and invoking false means of salvation, and at times has even seemed about to make them ashamed of themselves."[370] Dubois measures this difficulty not as a momentary response to contemporary events, but rather as a deep seated consequence of a long enduring system of injustice and oppression. He observes in particular implications of the abuse of black women on the culture, "The red stain of bastardy, which two centuries of systematic legal defilement of Negro women had stamped upon his race, meant not only the loss of ancient African chastity, but also the hereditary weight of a mass of corruption from white adulterers, threatening almost the obliteration of the Negro home."[371]

While the conditions that Dubois recounts were not swiftly developed, their contemporary import was undeniable, and cut right to the very valuation of the black person in America. On the one hand, those outside the community viewed

---

[369] Ibid.
[370] Ibid., 10.
[371] Ibid., 12.

them as half-human, and thus undeserving of the privileges of personhood, and on the other hand, having no hope within the community, there was little to strive for. Dubois echoes the painful cries, "Lo! we are diseased and dying, cried the dark hosts; we cannot write, our voting is vain; what need of education, since we must always cook and serve? And the Nation echoed and enforced this self-criticism, saying: Be content to be servants, and nothing more; what need of higher culture for half-men? Away with the black man's ballot, by force or fraud, – and behold the suicide of a race! "Nevertheless, out of the evil came something of good, – the more careful adjustment of education to real life, the clearer perception of the Negroes' social responsibilities, and the sobering realization of the meaning of progress."[372] While Dubois commendably finds some solace in that the pain of those times would help shape an approach to impacting culture, from a Biblical perspective the wounds were simply abhorrent and incompatible with the Divine expression of human valuation. It was not merely men and women who were violated – it was also their Creator.

Dubois further suggests that the "problem of the twentieth century is the problem of the color-line, – the relation of the darker to the lighter races of men in Asia and Africa, in America and the islands of the sea. It was a phase of this problem that caused the Civil War; and however much they who marched South and North in 1861 may have fixed on the technical points of union and local autonomy as a shibboleth, all nevertheless knew, as we know, that the question of Negro slavery was the real cause of the conflict."[373] The valuation

---

[372] Ibid., 13.
[373] Ibid., 15.

problem that had caused rift between brothers and sisters had manifest unsurprisingly in a national rift that shipwrecked a country and its people.

But once that conflict formally ended, there were great questions to be answered. Dubois retold history from the perspective of those who now had no place in society, were not yet fully treated as fully human, but were no longer either treated simply as property. What should be done with thousands of newly emancipated people? Dubois describes the governmental process of dealing with the "problem:" "Thus did the United States government definitely assume charge of the emancipated Negro as the ward of the nation. It was a tremendous undertaking. Here at a stroke of the pen was erected a government of millions of men, – and not ordinary men either, but black men emasculated by a peculiarly complete system of slavery, centuries old; and now, suddenly, violently, they come into a new birthright, at a time of war and passion, in the midst of the stricken and embittered population of their former masters."[374] This new cultural birth was traumatic, and did not bring with it the resolution of the valuation problem.

Lincoln's 1863 Emancipation Proclamation did not immediately provide its intended benefit. Dubois describes how the canyon grew between black and white post-Civil War, and how the government's efforts to establish and administer the Freedmen's Bureau was neither able to resolve some most basic problems, nor to ultimately quell enduring and growing racial tensions. As Dubois explains, the Bureau could do nothing other than fail: "In a time of perfect calm, amid willing neighbors and streaming wealth, the social uplifting of four million slaves to an

---

[374] Ibid., 20-21.

assured and self-sustaining place in the body politic and economic would have been a herculean task; but when to the inherent difficulties of so delicate and nice a social operation were added the spite and hate of conflict, the hell of war; when suspicion and cruelty were rife, and gaunt Hunger wept beside Bereavement, – in such a case, the work of any instrument of social regeneration was in large part fore-doomed to failure."[375] Dubois' concluding comment here is illustrative of the bigger reality in view – in the conditions symptomatic of a cursed and fallen creation, where the proper valuation of the Creator is not in view, and consequently *there is no remaining basis for the proper valuation of human life*, it is unsurprising that any instrument of social regeneration would be met with failure.

It is evident that the momentous progress that was made with the Proclamation had been engaged, at least by Lincoln's words as "an act of justice, warranted by the Constitution, upon military necessity...the considerate judgment of mankind, and the gracious favor of Almighty God."[376] That step of cultural progress was undertaken with the perspective of God as the Supreme Valuer, and thus the freeing of those He created *was* an act of justice. Still, that ontological acknowledgment did not change the hearts of men, nor their own individual perspectives on valuation. Dubois laments that "Slavery "classed the black man and the ox together. And the Negro knew full well that, whatever their deeper convictions may have been, Southern men had fought with desperate energy to perpetuate this slavery under which the black masses, with half-articulate thought, had

---

[375] Ibid., 25.
[376] Abraham Lincoln, "A Proclamation" January 1, 1863, viewed at https://www.archives.gov/exhibits/featured-documents/emancipation-proclamation/transcript.html.

writhed and shivered."[377] "So the cleft between the white and black South grew...it never should have been; it was as inevitable as its results were pitiable."[378]

Dubois reminds the reader that this wasn't merely a cultural phenomenon, *it was intensely personal.* Those that endured these times encountered dehumanizing torment to an incredible degree. Dubois reveals his own emotion at recounting the horrors, and explains with vivid clarity how both man and woman were scarred who lived through them:

> it is doubly difficult to write of this period calmly, so intense was the feeling, so mighty the human passions that swayed and blinded men. Amid it all, two figures ever stand to typify that day to coming ages, – the one, a gray-haired gentleman, whose fathers had quit themselves like men, whose sons lay in nameless graves; who bowed to the evil of slavery because its abolition threatened untold ill to all; who stood at last, in the evening of life, a blighted, ruined form, with hate in his eyes; – and the other, a form hovering dark and mother-like, her awful face black with the mists of centuries, had aforetime quailed at that white master's command, had bent in love over the cradles of his sons and daughters, and closed in death the sunken eyes of his wife, – aye, too, at his behest had laid herself low to his lust, and borne a tawny man-child to the world, only to see her dark boy's limbs scattered to the winds by midnight marauders riding after "cursed Niggers." These were the saddest

---

[377] Dubois, 25.
[378] Ibid., 25.

sights of that woful [sic] day; and no man clasped the hands of these two passing figures of the present-past; but, hating, they went to their long home, and, hating, their children's children live today.[379]

While Dubois recognizes that the Freedmen's Bureau saw success in the area of making education accessible (a victory that would have lasting impact), the Bureau was powerless to heal the scars Dubois exposes. Among other failures, the Bureau "failed to begin the establishment of good-will between ex-masters and freedmen, to guard its work wholly from paternalistic methods which discouraged self-reliance, and to carry out to any considerable extent its implied promises to furnish the freedmen with land."[380] "Its successes were the result of hard work, supplemented by the aid of philanthropists and the eager striving of black men. Its failures were the result of bad local agents, the inherent difficulties of the work, and national neglect."[381] Dubois identifies particular failures as if they might one day be remedied for future efforts. But the Biblicist might diagnose that those failures emanated from the same causative failures of every other economic and political enterprise designed to offset the symptoms of the spiritually dead human heart: *while the policies changed, the hearts of men had not.*

Despite its few successes, the numerous inadequacies of the Freedmen's Bureau illustrate the inherent deficiencies of governmental efforts to resolve deep-seated human problems. Whereas Leo XIII and Pius XI, Marx and Engels, and Gutiérrez

---

[379] Ibid., 26.
[380] Ibid., 29.
[381] Ibid., 29.

proposed economic solutions that as of yet have not resolved the problem, post-Civil War conditions in America showed that governments simply aren't equipped to address the issues that lead to the economic conditions that foster oppression. The problem is neither simply economic nor related to governance. The ongoing strife that Dubois exposed *is rooted simply in how individuals view their Creator, themselves, and others.*

In 1953 Dubois recognized that the color-line was symptomatic of an even greater problem: "I still think today as yesterday that the color-line is a great problem of this century. But today I see more clearly than yesterday that back of the problem of race and color, lies a greater problem which both obscures and implements it: and *that is the fact that so many civilized persons are willing to live in comfort even if the price of this is poverty, ignorance and disease of the majority of their fellowmen; that to maintain this privilege men have waged war until today war tends to become universal and continuous, and the excuse for this war continues largely to be color and race* [emphasis mine].[382]

While Dubois doesn't diagnose the problem as related directly to valuation, when considering this tragic episode of history, interlocutors would benefit from seeing through the Biblical lens, that all men being created equal is not the mere rhetoric of political calls to revolution, *but is representative of the Divine valuation of all human life as originating in God and thus constituting only one race,*[383] as bearing the image of God and thus bearing God-defined value,[384] as being reinforced in the prophetic hope of universal blessing covenanted by God to

---

[382] Ibid., 208.
[383] Genesis 1:27, 31.
[384] 1:26-27, 9:6.

Abraham,[385] and in the eschatological assurance that God would purchase those to be blessed from every tribe, tongue, people, and nation.[386]

MODEL 4 – THE MATTHEW 5-7 MODEL AND "EVERY TRIBE" INCLUSIVENESS

As Jesus began the public aspect of His earthly ministry, Matthew records Him as proclaiming and saying, "Repent for the kingdom of the heavens is at hand."[387] He traveled throughout the cities and villages and proclaimed "the gospel of the kingdom,"[388] and was healing many, demonstrating the validity of His messianic claim.[389] He acknowledges that part of His purpose for His sending was to accomplish that announcing of the kingdom.[390] The Sermon on the Mount offers in ten sections principles related to the coming kingdom. In this message Jesus (1) outlines the coming rewards (beatitudes) of the kingdom in 5:1-12, (2) describes how one enters the kingdom in 5:13-20, (3) contrasts authentic, internal righteousness with insufficient external righteousness in 5:21-47, (4) underscores the standard – the perfection of God the Father in 5:48, (5) distinguishes between the pursuit and temporal rewards of external righteousness and the pursuit and eternal rewards of kingdom-quality righteousness in 6:1-18, (6) exhorts the pursuit of eternal rewards in 6:19-24, (7) encourages in 6:25-34 that in

---

[385] Genesis 12:3b.
[386] Revelation 5:9.
[387] Matthew 4:17.
[388] 9:35.
[389] Luke 4:14-21.
[390] 4:43.

the pursuit of eternal reward there is present provision, (8) exposits in 7:1-14 the present character of kingdom-quality righteousness, (9) warns in 7:15-23 of the dangers of false fruit, and (10) illustrates in 7:24-29 by contrast the wisdom of building on solid foundation versus building on sand. In this Sermon is found a central and early portrait of the kingdom, and in this episode, Matthew records eight or nine direct mentions by Jesus of the kingdom, found in 5:3, 5:10, 5:19 (twice), 5:20, 6:10, 6:13 (in a textual variant), 6:33, and 7:21.

The 5:19 references relate to the abiding value of the Law, with future implications extending to the eschatological messianic kingdom: "Whoever then annuls one of the least of these commandments, and teaches others *to do* the same, shall be called least in the kingdom of heaven; but whoever keeps and teaches *them,* he shall be called great in the kingdom of heaven."[391] In 5:20, Jesus first draws the explicit contrast between inauthentic appearances of righteousness and the internal righteousness that is necessary for entrance into the kingdom: "For I say to you that unless your righteousness surpasses *that* of the scribes and Pharisees, you will not enter the kingdom of heaven."[392] In 6:10, Jesus teaches the disciples to pray, specifically to request that the kingdom of the heavens would come to earth as prophesied – a clear indication that it hadn't yet come: "Your kingdom come. Your will be done, On earth as it is in heaven."[393] In a textual variant[394] in the

---

[391] Matthew 5:19.

[392] 5:20.

[393] 6:10.

[394] "Several late manuscripts (157 225 418) append a trinitarian ascription, "for thine is the kingdom and the power and the glory of the Father and of the Son and of the Holy Spirit for ever. Amen." The same expansion occurs also at the close of the Lord's Prayer in the liturgy that

concluding portion of that same prayer, Jesus models the request in 6:13, "And do not lead us into temptation, but deliver us from evil. [For Yours is the kingdom and the power and the glory forever. Amen.]"[395] If authentic, this kingdom reference speaks of a present tense kingdom, but adds no earthly geographic implications to the revelation.

While the aforementioned passages (5:19, 5:20, 6:10, and 6:13) give no specific indicators beyond a general futuristic idea of a coming earthly kingdom, the beatitudes-preamble of 5:3-12 is explicitly eschatological with only three exceptions. Six of the nine identify future blessings associated with current conditional responsibilities. They include being comforted,[396] inheriting the earth,[397] being satisfied,[398] receiving mercy,[399] seeing God,[400] and being called sons of God.[401] The final of the beatitudes uses no verb, though it is still future looking, indicating the greatness of reward in heaven.

The first of the beatitudes, on the other hand, in 5:3, speaks of a presently held blessing: "Blessed are the poor in spirit, for theirs is (ἐστιν) the kingdom of heaven."[402] The

---

is traditionally ascribed to St. John Chrysostom. The absence of any ascription [is evident] in early and important representatives of the Alexandrian (ℵ B), the Western (D and most of the Old Latin), and other (f) types of text..." (Bruce Manning Metzger, United Bible Societies, *A Textual Commentary on the Greek New Testament, Second Edition a Companion Volume to the United Bible Societies' Greek New Testament (4th Rev. Ed.)* (London; New York: United Bible Societies, 1994), 14.)

[395] Matthew 6:13.

[396] 5:4.

[397] 5:5.

[398] 5:6.

[399] 5:7.

[400] 5:8.

[401] 5:9.

[402] 5:3.

penultimate beatitude likewise uses the same present tense phrasing in 5:10: "Blessed are those who have been persecuted for the sake of righteousness, for theirs is (ἐστιν) the kingdom of heaven."[403] While Jesus was proclaiming the kingdom as *being near* (ἤγγικεν),[404] He presented its possession *as a current reality*. How one understands the Author's usage of the present tense impacts the reader's understanding of social implications of the Sermon on the Mount.

On this context, Chafer illustrates what Hullinger refers to as the *kingdom view* interpretation of the Sermon:[405] "In this manifesto the King declares the essential character of the kingdom, the conduct which will be required in the kingdom, and the directions of entrance into the kingdom...when His kingdom was rejected and its realization delayed until the return of the King, the application of all Scripture which conditions life in the kingdom was delayed as well."[406] While through this lens the Sermon has secondary applications for today, the conditions are all future looking. In favor of a *disciple ethic* interpretation of the Sermon, Hullinger suggests "it could be successfully argued that the invitation at the end of the sermon regarding the narrow road is not an invitation to salvation as it is often presented, but rather, an invitation to Jesus' disciples to embrace the ethic he has expounded."[407] Hullinger's assertion is

---

[403] 5:10.

[404] 4:17.

[405] Jerry Hullinger, "Is There a "Dispensational" Approach to the Sermon on the Mount?" *1024 Project,* 2/17/2014, viewed at https://1024project.com/2014/02/17/is-there-a-dispensational-approach-to-the-sermon-on-the-mount/.

[406] Lewis Sperry Chafer, *Systematic Theology, 8 Volumes* (Dallas, TX: Dallas Seminary Press, 1948), 4:177-178.

[407] Hullinger, Ibid.

not incompatible with Chafer's future-fulfillment understanding and it complements Ryrie's assertion that all of the Sermon "has relevance for today."[408] While the future-looking beatitudes are evidence that Chafer is on the right theological track, the two that specifically address the kingdom in present tense terms indicate that there is more in view than simply the future physical arrival of the King in His kingdom.

George Eldon Ladd draws a similar conclusion in his assertion that "The Word of God *does* say that the Kingdom of God is a present spiritual reality,"[409] but Ladd goes too far in assigning geography to that present reality as "an inner spiritual redemptive blessing...present and at work in the world"[410] Ladd's already-not-yet theology is grounded in a geographically present (even if spiritual) manifestation of the kingdom within each believing individual. By contrast, Paul's instruction on the kingdom in the current age explicitly indicates different geographic parameters, as he reveals that God has "transferred *us* to the kingdom of His beloved Son."[411] It is evident that the kingdom doesn't change its location to the inner man, but rather the new creature is positionally transferred to the kingdom, hence, Paul's exhortation to "...keep seeking the things above, where Christ is, seated at the right hand of God. Set your mind on the things above, not on the things that are on earth. For you have died and your life is

---

[408] Charles Ryrie, *Dispensationalism Today* (Chicago, IL: Moody Press, 1969), 108.
[409] George Eldon Ladd, *The Gospel of the Kingdom* (), 16.
[410] Ladd, 18-19.
[411] Colossians 1:17.

hidden with Christ in God. When Christ, who is our life, is revealed, then you also will be revealed with Him in glory."[412]

D. Martin Lloyd Jones takes Ladd's geographical leap to its logical conclusion when he asserts that "the kingdom of God is in every true Christian. He reigns in the Church when she acknowledges Him truly. The kingdom has come, the kingdom is coming, the kingdom is yet to come. Now we must always bear that in mind. Whenever Christ is enthroned as King, the kingdom of God is come, so that, while we cannot say that He is ruling over all in the world at the present time, He is certainly ruling in that way in the hearts and lives of all His people"[413] If Christ is presently ruling on the throne, as is asserted by already-not-yet, amillennial, and postmillennial models, then the kingdom is here and should be expected to generate kingdom results.

Gentry and Wellum directly connect the Biblical covenants to God's plan for kingdom results in the form of social justice, characterizing Israel, "As a community in covenant relationship to Yahweh, they are called to mirror to the world the character of Yahweh in terms of social justice and to be a vehicle of blessing and salvation to the nations."[414] After Israel's failure to fulfill that calling, "The Lord will establish Zion as the people/place where all nations will seek his instruction for social justice."[415] Yet even after return from exile, "the failure to

---

[412] *New American Standard Bible: 1995 Update* (La Habra, CA: The Lockman Foundation, 1995), Col 3:1–4.

[413] D. Martin Lloyd Jones, *Studies in the Sermon on the Mount* (Grand Rapids, MI: Eerdmans, 1984), 16.

[414] Peter Gentry and Stephen Wellum, *Kingdom Through Covenant: A Biblical Theological Understanding of the Covenants, 2nd Edition* (Wheaton, IL: Crossway, 2018), 436.

[415] Gentry and Wellum, 437.

practice social justice remains a central problem."[416] Despite these failings, "Both social justice and faithful loyal love are expressions of the character of Yahweh and of conduct expected in the covenant community where Yahweh is king,"[417] and thus "A coming Davidic king...will perfectly represent the Lord by implementing social justice..."[418] That kingdom is manifest in the current church: "The *newness* of the church is a redemptive-historical newness, rooted in the coming of Christ and the inauguration of the new covenant. In him, all of the previous covenants, which in type, shadow and prophetic announcement anticipated and foreshadowed him have now come to their *telos*."[419]

The assertions by Gentry and Wellum underscore the practical appeal of already-not-yet, postmillennial, and amillennial interpretations of the Sermon. The ethical implications are further illustrated by David Jones' kingdom-now assertion that, "As the kingdom of God grows, then the gospel gradually counteracts and corrects the effects of sin in the world through the process of restoration and reconciliation...the gospel is no less comprehensive than the fall..."[420] The realized eschatology interpretations of the Sermon on the Mount, with kingdom present both in time and space provide a compelling ethical foundation for contemporary social justice engagement and lend support to the economic and political ideologies

---

[416] Ibid., 438.
[417] Ibid., 582.
[418] Ibid., 643.
[419] Ibid., 685.
[420] David Jones, *Introduction to Biblical Ethics* (Nashville: TN, B&H Academic, 2013), 64.

espoused by Leo XIII and Pius XI, and Gutiérrez, and even Marx and Engels (atheism not withstanding).

On the other hand, reading the Sermon and other kingdom passages of Matthew through the normative literal grammatical historical hermeneutic (LGH) helps the reader understand as did Toussaint, that, "The kingdom exists in the intercalation only in the sense that the sons of the kingdom are present. But strictly speaking the kingdom of the heavens...refers to the prophesied and coming kingdom on earth."[421] The exhortation of 6:33 is an important echo of 5:3 and 5:10, to that end: "But seek first His kingdom and His righteousness, and all these things will be added to you."[422] While there is a future tense promise (προστεθήσεται), there is a present tense responsibility (ζητεῖτε). This supports the model Chafer and Ryrie advocated, and brings to focus an important principle: *there is no theological necessity for realized eschatology in order to justify a vibrant sense of contemporary responsibility.* The mandate to seek first the kingdom and its righteousness has nothing whatsoever with the timing of the actual coming of the kingdom. Jesus' listeners were to be seeking that kingdom and its characteristic righteousness *even when the kingdom wasn't present in any fulfillment sense.* Likewise, the Sermon's final kingdom reference in 7:21 emphasizes the present tense responsibility (ποιῶν) for a future entering into (εἰσελεύσεται) the kingdom: "Not everyone who says to Me, 'Lord, Lord,' will enter the kingdom of heaven, but he who does the will of My Father who is in heaven *will enter.*"[423] The one

---

[421] Stanley Toussaint, *Behold the King: A Study of Matthew* (Portland, OR: Multnomah, 1980), 172.
[422] Matthew 6:33.
[423] Matthew 7:21.

doing His will in the present will enter the kingdom at some future point in time.

CONCLUSION

While realized eschatology models offer easy motivation for social justice because of their integral assertions that the kingdom is already here, the LGH derived understanding that eschatology has not been realized does not at all minimize present responsibility. In fact, such a perspective makes the responsibility perhaps even clearer. Rather than asserting some mystery form of the kingdom and claiming a tangible manifestation when there simply isn't any, the mere fact that believers are actually citizens of a not-yet-here kingdom and that they are *told* to seek first the righteousness of that kingdom provides an explicit higher-order mandate.

When that kingdom is physically relocated to earth, then the promise of universal blessing through Abraham, given in Genesis 12:3b will be tangible reality. When that kingdom is physically relocated to earth, we will behold "a great multitude which no one could count, from every nation and *all* tribes and peoples and tongues,"[424] While this is a heavenly multitude in Revelation 7:9, their geography changes in Revelation 19. God's original promise to Abraham, and His covenant program expressed through the subsequent covenants is brought to fruition in the reign of Jesus Christ at the arrival of His kingdom of the heavens *on earth* (hence, Matthew's verbiage), and the ushering in of eternity that soon follows.

---

[424] Revelation 7:9.

If that certain kingdom future reflects an enduring unity of nation, tribe, people, and tongue, then in the present seeking the kingdom and its righteousness, we are building houses on the rock – a present activity with enduring result. If one enduring condition (even though not in any way brought on by our efforts) includes the unity of nation, tribe, people, and tongue, then our present activity should be characterized by things that reflect that eschatological progress. Biblical ethics in the church age corroborate this concept as we are to honor all people,[425] treating others as worthy of more honor than ourselves.[426] We are to do good to all, not only of the household of faith, though especially to those of the household of faith.[427] We are "to malign no one, to be peaceable, gentle, showing every consideration for all men."[428]

It is worth noting that among the reasons Paul offers for that last mandate, is that *we too were formerly enslaved.*[429] Certainly, the enslavement to which Paul refers is not the kind which Dubois laments, but enslavement of any human derivation keeps us from living as our Creator designed. Should we not demonstrate the newness of thinking exemplified by Paul when he referred to Onesimus as no longer a slave, but a beloved brother?[430] Paul expresses present-tense kingdom love when he exhorts Philemon to "accept [Onesimus] as me,"[431] and in so doing Philemon would be refreshing Paul's heart in Christ.[432]

---

[425] 1 Peter 2:17.
[426] Philippians 2:1-11.
[427] Galatians 6:10.
[428] Titus 3:2.
[429] 3:3.
[430] Philemon 16.
[431] 17.
[432] 20.

If believers are *"willing to live in comfort even if the price of this is poverty, ignorance and disease of the majority of their fellowmen,"*[433] even continually waging war "to maintain this privilege,"[434] as Dubois asserts, then how can we claim to be imitating Paul as he imitates Christ?[435] Are such injustices capable of being met with the ideologies of Marx and Engels, Leo XIII and Pius XI, and Gutiérrez? Or might we recognize that Christ mandated, in the Sermon on the Mount, *a future-looking perspective that had clear present-day applications*? Might we fix our gaze on what Paul highlights, in Philippians 2:1-11 – the example of Jesus Christ as modeling both the future-focus and the right-now striving? We don't need to manipulate hermeneutic methods, contrive theological fictions, nor seek economic and political saviors in order to advocate for a strong commitment to social justice (as defined by the Creator). While the particulars of *how* to best express and apply that commitment might be open to debate, that *the Bible requires such a commitment in this present age of those who would follow Jesus* is not.

---

[433] Dubois, 208.
[434] Ibid.
[435] 1 Corinthians 4:16, 11:1.

CHAPTER 9
THE INSUFFICIENCY OF CRITICAL RACE THEORY[436]

Richard Delgado and Jean Stefancic perceive Critical Race Theory (CRT) to be a hermeneutic issue at its core, "From critical legal studies, the group borrowed the idea of legal indeterminacy – the idea that not every legal case has one correct outcome. Instead, one can decide most cases either way, by emphasizing one line of authority over another, or interpreting one fact differently from the way one's adversary does."[437] Beginning from a vantage point of division and viewing elements of society through the oppressed/oppressor lens, CRT works from the assumption that society is broken, needs analysis, and needs systematic repair. In all three of these aspects there is merit, and no one should be afraid of looking into nooks and crannies and the hidden corners of society to discover the root causes of inequality.

Unfortunately, Delgado and Stefancic seem to focus CRT primarily on Marxist economic concepts and disregard some of

---

[436] Adapted from "A Biblical Model for Race Reconciliation" in *Applied Biblical Worldview: Essays on Christian Ethics* (Fort Worth, TX: Exegetica Publishing, 2016), 265-271.

[437] Richard Delgado and Jean Stafancic, Critical Race Theory: An Introduction (New York: New York University Press, 2001), 4-5.

the obvious history that gives way to the oppression they cite. The economic examination is helpful, but only if we diagnose correctly the problem that leads to the economic situation. That problem is no more evident than in the writings of Democratic Senator Theodore Bilbo. In the late 1940's Bilbo wrote a book entitled *Take Your Choice: Separation or Mongrelization,*[438] which argued for purity of the races. He suggested that both black and white should wish to maintain segregation in order to protect their distinct races. Bilbo illustrated how important racial purity was to him, saying,

> Personally, the writer of this book would rather see his race and his civilization blotted out with the atomic bomb than to see it slowly but surely destroyed in the maelstrom of miscegenation, interbreeding, intermarriage and mongrelization. The destruction in either case would be inevitable - one in a flash and the other by the slow but certain process of sin, degradation, and mongrelization.[439]

Bilbo's sentiment was not uncommon in his day, and even in this one there are voices of agreement. But where does Bilbo's "purity" concept come from? What is the root of this desire for racial separateness? His use of the Bible provides some help in answering the question. Bilbo justifies the segregation idea as rooted in God's own design:

---

[438] Theodore Bilbo, *Take Your Choice: Separation or Mongrelization* (Poplarville, MS: Dreamhouse Publishers, 1947).
[439] Bilbo, Preface.

The fact that God did ordain the division of the people of the earth into separate races as a part of the Divine plan is sufficient for our purpose...God saw fit to segregate and separate the different races by placing each in different lands. He located the white races in the middle northern hemisphere, and placed the Negro in Africa, and the brown and yellow peoples in other spheres, as far as possible from each other. He divided them by color lines as well as by territorial lines so that each race would maintain its racial integrity.[440]

In Bilbo's view, God set the distinctions, thus to "mix and mingle and intermarry with white people" is "to defy the laws of God and man."[441] Consequently, the contemporary struggles to advance segregation were justified, in the minds of Bilbo and others. Bilbo illustrates this when he asks, "Since God set the example, why should Southerners be so severely criticized for following His footsteps?"

What Bilbo is referring to as God's ordaining of the division is found in Genesis 11. In this chapter, all humanity had failed to obey God's command to "be fruitful and multiply and fill the earth."[442] Instead they were remaining in one place, lest they "be scattered over the face of the whole earth." God confused their language "so that they will not understand one another's speech."[443] It is clear from the context that this scattering had to do with forcing humanity to obey God's earlier command and thwarting human attempts at centralizing (in

---

[440] Bilbo, Chapter 6.
[441] Bilbo, Chapter 6.
[442] Genesis 9:1.
[443] Genesis 11:7.

this case in direct disobedience to God). Unlike as in Bilbo's interpretation, this division had absolutely nothing to do with race. It was the languages that were confused, not the skin colors, and not the blood.

Bilbo proclaims that, "nothing is more sacred than racial integrity. Purity of race is a gift of God. But it is a gift which man can destroy. And God, in his infinite wisdom, has so ordained it that when man destroys his racial purity, it can never be redeemed." Yet there is no Scripture that would agree with the statement that purity of race is a gift of God, nor that racial integrity is sacred. These are not Biblical concepts.

Bilbo even appeals to Jesus as a supporter of separateness: "Racial integrity and the purity of the blood are in accordance with the teachings of Jesus Christ who set the standards for high and noble living some two thousand years ago."[444] Yet again, there is no statement of Jesus that can be used to support these assertions.

Bilbo moves further into the NT, explaining that Paul shouldn't be interpreted literally, lest we misunderstand how God intends us to handle race: "Paul's statement that God "hath made of one blood all nations of men for to dwell on the face of the earth' is as much spiritual as his other statement that God "dwelleth not in temples made with hands" and his assurance that the Lord "be not far from every one of us, for in him we live, and move, and have our being...for we are also his offspring." It may also be pointed out that in the same verse which made reference to the "one blood" of all nations of men, the great Disciple said that God "hath determined...the bounds of their habitation." Until some men migrated and others were moved

---

[444] Bilbo, Chapter 8.

by force by their conquerors, who can say that it was not in the Divine scheme of things that the different races should be on the separate continents with physical barriers to prevent their intermingling?"

Specifically, Bilbo is referencing Acts 17:26, in which Paul addressing the men of Athens explains how God is worthy of worship and how He had interacted with humanity in Jesus Christ. Bilbo emphasizes Paul's mention that God has "established the boundaries of their habitation" as a design for racial separateness. Clearly, Paul has no racial issues in mind, as he agrees with the Athenian poets who said, "For we are also His children."[445] Further, Paul presents the universal need and opportunity for repentance.[446] Later Paul would explain that all are in need of salvation,[447] it is a universal reality that crosses racial distinctions.

Bilbo seeks to protect the races from intermarriage that would destroy their uniqueness, and he offers an interpretation of history that would agree with the negative impact of intermarriage. He concludes that viewing intermarriage positively doesn't allow for a proper view of God:

> Those who are attempting to implant the doctrine of social equality of the races throughout this land and seeking to promote the intermarriage of the races must indeed think that Almighty God, the Creator of the heavens and the earth, made a mistake...[448]

---

[445] Acts 17:28.
[446] 17:30.
[447] Romans 1:17-20.
[448] Bilbo, Chapter 8.

According to Bilbo, there are sobering consequences for viewing God this way. Engaging in any joining of the races is highly problematic:

> The very fact that separate and distinct races of mankind have been created makes it impossible for anyone to claim that God did not ordain the racial distinction. When man breaks the laws of God and brings about the mixing of the blood of the different races, he and his posterity will pay the penalty.[449]

Bilbo wants America to avoid this penalty, and thus advocates strongly for segregation and racial separateness. The logical conclusion of Bilbo's views, played out especially in the last two centuries of American history, is oppression and disunity. I find Bilbo's error symptomatic of three deeper failures.

First, Bilbo has a theological precommitment favoring segregation and racial separateness, so when he invokes the Bible he does not do so in a literal grammatical historical way. In other words, he is not handling the text objectively, but rather he is reading into the text concepts that are entirely foreign to it. Bilbo has failed to interpret the Bible well, and has made it say things it doesn't say, and in so doing has made God the scapegoat for Bilbo's errant views. The Biblical God is not a racist. Certainly, He commanded Israel to remain separate from the nations around it – even avoiding intermarrying with them. But this was for very specific reason having nothing to do with blood and race: "For they will turn your sons away from

---

[449] Bilbo, Chapter 12.

following me to serve other gods..."[450] Bilbo doesn't acknowledge that purpose, nor does he acknowledge that God's commands in this context were for Israel alone, and not for America or any other nation.

Second, Bilbo perceives Darwin as a great scientist, along with Spencer, Haeckel, Mendel, and Pearson – particularly in discussing the power of heredity. Bilbo betrays a Darwinian assessment on racial superiority. Darwin's *On the Origin of Species by Means of Natural Selection or the Preservation of Favoured Races in the Struggle for Life* went a long way in encouraging humanity in the view that some races were "favoured" genetically over others. Even Darwin's own experience in viewing "savage" peoples caused him to view his own culture as so far superior that the two groups could have only distant relation. Darwin once remarked, "Viewing such men, one can hardly make one's self believe that they are fellow-creatures, and inhabitants of the same world...Whilst beholding these savages, one asks, whence have they come? What could have tempted, or what change compelled a tribe of men, to leave the fine regions of the north...? I believe, in this extreme part of South America, man exists in a lower state of improvement than in any other part of the world."[451] The inferiority of races is a Darwinian idea, not a Biblical one.

Finally, Bilbo – like all of us – is beset by the selfish, envious, and dark flaws of fallen human nature. "The heart is more deceitful than all else, and is desperately sick; who can understand it?"[452] When we hold views that elevate us over

---

450 Deuteronomy 7:4.
451 Charles Darwin, *The Voyage of the Beagle*, edited by Charles Eliot (New York: PF Collier and Sons, 1909), 228-246.
452 Jeremiah 17:9.

others, we are being deceived by our own brokenness. James offers a simple warning to believers that we are not to "hold your faith in our glorious Lord Jesus with an attitude of personal favoritism."[453] James also identifies the source of our disunity and conflicts: "What is the source of quarrels and conflicts among you? Is not the source your pleasures that wage war in your members? You lust and do not have; so you commit murder. You are envious and cannot obtain; so you fight and quarrel."[454] The problem is our own brokenness. The solution James prescribes is to "Submit therefore to God…Humble yourselves in the presence of God and He will exalt you."[455] Paul echoes these words in Philippians 2:3, when he says, "Do nothing from selfishness or empty conceit, but with humility of mind regard one another as more important than yourselves." To suggest that one race is superior to another is an empty conceit. How can we possibly regard one another as more important than ourselves if we are claiming that we are more important than others? These are mutually exclusive ideas.

Better to serve one another, to love one another, in honor of our Lord who died and rose again so that all who believe in Him might have eternal life. Let us never forget that people of all races will dwell together forever.

> For God has not destined us for wrath, but for obtaining
> salvation through our Lord Jesus Christ, who died for us,
> so that whether we are awake or asleep, **we will live**

---

[453] James 2:1.
[454] James 4:1-2a.
[455] James 4:7a, 10.

together with Him. Therefore encourage one another and build up one another, just as you also are doing.[456]

---

[456] 1 Thessalonians 5:9-11.

CHAPTER 10
IS CHRISTIANITY BAD FOR THE ENVIRONMENT?
A BIBLICAL VIEW
OF ENVIRONMENTAL RESPONSIBILITY[457]

The climate changed (pun intended) dramatically in 1966 when medieval historian Lynn White presented a groundbreaking paper to the American Association for the Advancement of Science. The paper was well received and was published a few months later in the 155th volume of the academic journal, *Science*. White's paper, "The Historical Roots of our Ecological Crisis," was a scathing critique of what he understood to be the Judeo-Christian attitude toward nature. White laid the blame particularly on Christianity for what was understood at the time to be a global ecological crisis. "Historical Roots" set the tone for environmental philosophy, and since that publication, Christianity has been perceived within the environmental movement as public enemy number one. One scholar even suggested that "the culpability of Christianity in the destruction of the natural world and the uselessness of Christianity in any

---

[457] Published as Christopher Cone, "Is Christianity Bad for the Environment" in the *Regular Baptist Bulletin*, Sept/Oct '19.

effort to correct that destruction are now established clichés of the conservation movement.[458]

Specifically, White accused Christianity of being the most anthropocentric (man-centered) religion the world has ever seen. He thought that the Judeo-Christian creation account placed all of nature at human disposal, and that God mandated that there would be no other purpose for nature but to serve human purposes. Consequently, White suggested, humanity abused nature, and believed they were doing so with God's permission. Was Lynn White correct? Is Christianity to blame for environmental problems? Or perhaps White has misunderstood Christianity and failed to recognize the environmental responsibility the Bible prescribes.

THE IMPORTANCE OF PRESUPPOSITIONS

The late Carl Sagan, famed astronomer, evolutionary thinker, and environmental scientist, began his bestselling book *Cosmos* with the assertion that, "The Cosmos is all that is or ever was or ever will be."[459] He concludes the book by saying,

> ...we are the local embodiment of a Cosmos grown to self awareness. We have begun to contemplate our origins: starstuff pondering the stars; organized assemblages of ten billion billion billion atoms considering the evolution of atoms; tracing the long journey by which, here at least, consciousness arose. Our loyalties are to the species and the planet. We speak for Earth. Our obligation to survive

[458] Wendell Berry, "Christianity and the Survival of Creation" in Seeing God Everywhere, Barry McDonald, ed. (World Wisdom, 2004), 53.
[459] Carl Sagan, Cosmos (New York, NY: Ballantine, 1980), 1.

is owed not just to ourselves but also to that Cosmos, ancient and vast, from which we spring.[460]

Logically flowing from Sagan's statement of faith is a statement of worship: the cosmos is the only ever-existing reality, thus we owe our loyalty to the cosmos. While Sagan was an avowed atheist, he demonstrated remarkable faith, proclaiming the gospel of the cosmos. It is interesting that Sagan and others sharing his view adhere to at least the fundamental elements of a religious system. There is content of faith (the cosmos as eternal reality), worship is the reasonable obligation of that faith (loyalties owed to the cosmos), and there is revelation that helps seekers to understand the intricacies of that faith (the prophetic material of Sagan's *Cosmos*).

Obviously, Bible believers can not share Sagan's faith, since it directly contradicts much revealed in the Bible. In particular, the premise that there is no transcendent and personal God undermines the very possibility of the Bible having any authority over human behavior. If Sagan's presupposition (that the Cosmos is eternal reality) should be rejected, then shouldn't his conclusion – that we owe loyalty to the cosmos – also be rejected? Sagan justifies his environmental agenda based on his statement of faith. If we reject Sagan's statement of faith – which is the basis for the secular understanding of environmental responsibility – then how should Christians understand their relationship to nature? If Bible believers do not acknowledge human debt to the cosmos, then isn't Lynn White correct in his accusations?

---

[460] Sagan, 286.

White suggested that at the ground level the Judeo-Christian system has got it all wrong, even though he admits limited knowledge of the true cause of or severity of the crisis. He says, "The history of ecological change is still so rudimentary that we know little about what really happened, or what the results were."[461] "What shall we do? No one yet knows."[462] Though uncertain of the severity of the problem, he blames "the presuppositions that underlie modern technology and science"[463] and suggests the current crisis is "the product of an emerging, entirely novel, democratic culture. The issue is whether a democratized world can survive its own implications. Presumably we cannot unless we rethink our axioms."[464] So, which presuppositions does White vilify?

> Since both our technological and our scientific movements got their start, acquired their character, and achieved world dominance in the Middle Ages, it would seem that we cannot understand their nature or their present impact upon ecology without examining medieval assumptions and developments.[465]

White asserts that modern technology is rooted in ruthlessness toward nature.

He traces this ruthlessness to the view that "man and nature are two things, and man is master,"[466] and he suggests

---

461 Lynn Townsend White, Jr, "The Historical Roots of Our Ecological Crisis", Science, Vol 155 (Number 3767), March 1967, pp. 1203-1207.
462 White, 1204.
463 White, 1204.
464 White, 1204.
465 White, 1204-1205.
466 White, 1205.

that the source of this view is religion, but not just any religion: "The victory of Christianity over paganism was the greatest psychic revolution in the history of our culture."[467] No longer did people believe that trees had spirits, for example, now they were merely resources to be used for human consumption. White concludes that, "We shall continue to have a worsening ecologic crisis until we reject the Christian axiom that nature has no reason for existence save to serve man."[468] Was White correct in suggesting that this was actually a Christian axiom?

In fact, White was not correct, if Christian doctrine is derived from the Bible. The axiom that "nature has no reason for exist save to serve man" is directly contradicted by the Bible itself. Note for example that the works of God directly identified in Scripture all are said to serve His own purpose of demonstrating His glory:

> The major works of God revealed in Scripture *all* serve the doxological purpose (Ps. 86:9-10; Rev. 15:4); as a matter of fact, Scripture identifies no greater purpose for each of the following: God's Predestining and Calling Works (Eph. 1:5-12; 2 Pet. 1:3); the Ministry of Christ (Jn. 13:31-2; 17:1-5; 21:19; 2 Cor. 1:20; Heb. 13:21); Creation (Ps. 19; Is. 40; Rev. 4:11); the Keeping of His word (Rom. 3:1-7); Salvation (Ps. 79:9; Rom. 15:7; 16:25-27; Eph. 1:14; 1 Tim. 1:15-17; 2 Tim. 4:18; Jude 24-25); the church (1 Cor. 10:31; 2 Cor. 4:15; Eph. 1:12; Php. 1:11; 2 Thess. 1:11-12; 1 Pet. 4:11,16); fruitfulness of believers (Jn. 15:8; 1 Cor. 10:31); the kingdom (Php. 2:11; 1 Thess. 2:12; Rev.

---

[467] White, 1205.
[468] White, 1207.

1:6); sickness, death, and resurrection (1 Sam. 6:5; Lk. 17:11-18; Jn. 9:1-3; 11:4); judgment (Rom. 3:7; Rev. 14:7); deliverance of Israel (Is. 60:21; 61:3); and the fulfilling of covenants and summing up of all things (Is. 25:1-3; 43:20; Lk. 2:14; Rom. 4:20; 15:8-9; 2 Cor. 1:20; 2 Pet. 1:3-4; Rev. 19:7).[469]

While each of these works of God certainly do often provide great benefits for humanity, they are described in the Scriptures as serving God's purposes, not those of mankind. White says, "Christianity is the most anthropocentric religion the world has seen,"[470] but that doesn't square with the Biblical record either. Based on God's revealed purpose of expressing His own glory, the Bible is *overwhelmingly theocentric* (God-centered), and not anthropocentric. It seems evident that White did not base his critiques on what the Bible *actually says*. (Actually, White was perhaps unwittingly critiquing the Western tradition that was more rooted in Catholicism than the Bible itself, though he does speak poorly of the creation account as recorded in Genesis.) Especially for people who desire to think Biblically, we need to know what the Bible actually says.

WHAT DOES THE BIBLE SAY ABOUT ENVIRONMENTAL RESPONSIBILITY?

Genesis 1:26-28 includes what is often referred to as the dominion mandate. The verb *radah* (1:26) is appropriately translated as *rule* or *dominate*. This dominion mandate, or

---

[469] Christopher Cone, *Prolegomena: Introductory Notes on Bible Study & Theological Method* (Fort Worth, TX: Tyndale Seminary Press, 2008), 7.
[470] White, 1205.

cultural mandate, was given to perfect and sinless man who was qualified as God's representative to properly govern the earth. The perspective that considers the dominion mandate to be God's abiding marching orders for all of humanity and their relationship to nature is often referred to as *dominionism*. It is dominionism in particular that Lynn White critiqued. Based on the account in Genesis 2, some see a *stewardship ethic*. This is perhaps a kinder, gentler version of dominionism, in that Adam is not portrayed in Genesis 2 as dominating nature, but rather as stewarding creation.

But neither the dominionist nor the stewardship model fully account for the impact of the Fall. As humanity was created in the image of God, God declares that His creation, including mankind, was very good (1:31). However, the sin recorded in Genesis 3 resulted in a changed condition for humanity and all of creation. Mankind was no longer qualified to govern creation, as evidenced by: (1) the curse that came to the earth as a result of Adam's governance (3:17), (2) increased difficulty in working with the earth (3:17), (3) finite lifespan that would make discovery of nature far more difficult (3:19), and most importantly, (4) the image of God in man was now altered or augmented by the image of Adam – of fallen man (5:3). God's description in Genesis 6:5 of the human condition is certainly no endorsement of human qualification for governing the earth: "Then the Lord saw that the wickedness of man was great on the earth, and that every intent of the thoughts of his heart was only evil continually." (6:5)

After God judges the world through the flood and begins anew with Noah and his family, God repeats the "be fruitful and multiply" imperative (c.f., 1:28 and 9:7), but *omits entirely any discussion of ruling or subduing*. Clearly, humanity has lost both the ability and the privilege to govern. In order for humanity even to survive, God institutes in Genesis 9:6 a sanctity-of-life ethic expressed in capital punishment. He also places the fear of humanity in animals so that they might not destroy mankind (9:2,5), and He covenants with all living things (9:12) that He will not again judge the world by flood (9:11).

We learn from the first nine chapters of Genesis that humanity is not only incapable of governing creation, but even needs divine accommodation just to survive. We don't rule and subdue the earth – on the contrary, the earth fights back, and ultimately wins, as people return in death to the dust from whence we came. The dominion mandate was given to the innocent humanity, and no longer applies – that is why the dominion mandate is *redacted*. Dominion is given in 1:26-28. The judgment after the Fall in Genesis 3 reminds us that the earth would not be cooperative. Genesis 9:7 repeats the "be fruitful and multiply" command but omits the "rule and subdue" imperative. Thorns, thistles, and humanity returning to dust reminds us that things in this life are broken, and the solution isn't found in our capacity to rule over nature.

If we operate with the idea that we have dominion today, then we aren't aligning with the Genesis account, and one common byproduct of that kind of thinking is the anthropocentrism that Lynn White critiques. Wouldn't it also be incredibly arrogant of us to suggest we can redeem God's creation when we are in need of redemption ourselves? Historically, nothing good comes from us exalting ourselves, and it would serve us well to remember Paul's exhortation in Philippians 2 that we not think more highly of ourselves than we ought. It is ironic that non-biblical models for environmental responsibility all share in common the ideal that humanity can be the saviors of the cosmos. The Biblical approach crushes that concept, destroying anthropocentrism, and providing a reliable environmental ethic. There are quite a few environmental ethics models that attempt to topple man-centered thinking, but only the Biblical model effectively resolves the problem.

According to the Bible, we live in and are part of God's creation. The universe around us was all made and is all held together for His own glory, and we each play small roles in His plan. We have no value in and of ourselves; our only value is found in the fact that He created us in His image, and He intends for us to participate in His plan to express His own glory. Because we are sinners, born into brokenness, falling short of His glory, and separated from Him, we are not qualified to govern or steward His creation. All of creation groans under the weight of sin and awaits the redemption only He can provide.[471]

Because of what He has done and what He will do, we can have confidence in the simple instructions He provided. They help us understand our environmental responsibility as ultimately our *responsibility to Him.* While the Bible provides us with far more than simply an environmental guidebook, it does give us a straightforward approach to environmental responsibility: Instead of pridefully stepping into the role of redeemers, we are commissioned to walk in simple and humble obedience to our God.[472] We are exhorted to avoid the greed that leads to the abuse of God's resources,[473] not because we worship those resources, and not because we view them as ours, but because we are commanded to honor the One to whom they truly

---

[471] Romans 8:18-25.
[472] Micah 6:8.
[473] Ephesians 4:19-20.

belong – remember, the earth is the Lord's and all it contains.[474] We are asked to avoid the selfishness that leads to apathy and shortsightedness,[475] and that causes us not to consider the difficulties and needs of those less fortunate than we.[476] We are challenged to avoid cruelty towards God's creatures.[477] Cruelty shows that we are only concerned for our conveniences and is symptomatic of a failure to recognize that they are indeed *His creatures*. God cares about His creatures and establishes guidelines for their care.[478] Ultimately, we are urged to avoid the self-exaltation of man-centered thinking and to think and behave from a *theocentric* perspective. God is at the center, not us![479]

We should be focused on things above where our Lord is seated,[480] and in doing so we should not use our heavenly home as an excuse to have poor manners as guests in the earthly house that God has provided. In this sense, we are stewards. As Paul exhorts, while we have opportunity, we should be doing good to all.[481] Caring properly for the world around us, for example, benefits others and is an act of worship of the Creator.

In order to do these things well, we need to recognize that God's word is reliable and provides us what we need to confront any problems – even ecological ones.[482] When we understand the Bible to communicate what the Author intended, we don't need

---

[474] Psalm 24:1.
[475] Romans 6:6.
[476] Proverbs 22:9.
[477] Proverbs 12:10.
[478] For example, 1 Timothy 5:18.
[479] Revelation 22:13, Job 38:4, 12, and 35, and John 3:30, for example.
[480] Colossians 3:1-4.
[481] Galatians 6:10.
[482] 2 Timothy 3:16-17, 2 Peter 1:3.

to be afraid to engage in public discourse on environmental responsibility or any other topic. Of course, we don't expect to be praised by a world that views His word as foolishness, but still we should not disengage or hide from the world the principles and solutions that God provides in His word. He tells us not just how to deal with symptoms, but He tells us how to understand and access the remedy for the disease itself. The disease isn't simply an ecological crisis, but it is first and foremost a spiritual crisis that has many destructive manifestations in the world around us. The disease of sin can only be cured by the grace of God through faith in Jesus Christ. If we ignore the symptoms, then we are poor stewards, missing opportunities to show God's love and compassion to His creation around us. If we ignore the disease itself, then we fail at one of the greatest stewardships He has provided us – the privilege of presenting the cure, namely reconciliation to God.[483] If we live daily from a theocentric perspective as the Bible prescribes, we will be better at prioritizing according to what God prioritizes, and we will be less focused on our own wants and concerns, and more concerned about how God wants us to interact with Him, with other people, and with His creation.

Rather than look to the Bible, Lynn White recommends we look to Francis of Assisi as the patron saint for ecologists because Francis "tried to depose man from his monarchy over creation and set up a democracy of all God's creatures."[484] I would suggest that John the Baptist provided a better roadmap than did Francis, for environmental (and every other kind of) responsibility, when John said, "He must increase, but I must

---

[483] 2 Corinthians 5:20.
[484] White, 1206.

decrease."[485] John understood that the issue is not about a democracy of creatures, but rather a monarchy of God as sovereign over all of His creation. God is at the center. Properly relating with any aspect of God's creation begins with properly relating to Him. Perhaps one could even say that because Biblical Christianity prescribes a theocentric manner of thought and behavior, Biblical Christianity has nothing whatsoever to do with causing any ecological crisis but is instead a great benefit to the environment. Our Creator knows how to properly employ His creation, and we can trust His direction.

---

[485] John 3:30.

CHAPTER 11
GRACE IN POLITICS: A BIBLICAL MODEL FOR EFFECTIVE POLITICAL ENGAGEMENT

Edgar Allen Poe once said that "In one case out of a hundred a point is excessively discussed because it is obscure; in the ninety-nine remaining it is obscure because it is excessively discussed." At the height of socio-political discourse, the bases for key ideas often become obscure as outcomes and not foundations are more readily at the center of conversation. This chapter considers foundations for socio-political discussion by examining Biblical narratives engaging political contexts in order to help us (1) identify Biblical norms for political speech and action (2) deal with failure, division, and disunity, and (3) understand how grace should shape our political engagement.

BIBLICAL NORMS FOR POLITICAL SPEECH AND ACTION

The most comprehensive discussions of interaction with government are found in Romans 13:1-7 and 1 Peter 2:13-20. These passages share much commonality and make several important principles evident. First, Paul asserts that authorities are appointed by God, and thus subjection of those under that authority is universal.[486] There is a differentiation between authority and rulers,[487] though that distinction should not be evident in practicality. It is assumed that rulers would be fulfilling their responsibility as designed.[488] These rulers are ministers of God for good to those in subjection,[489] but if they are not ruling that way, there is no recourse in this passage for the governed. The relationship between the governors and the governed is necessarily based on the mutual goodness of the governors and willing subjection by the governed. As is the case in other relationship structures in Scripture[490] there is no provision made for either party failing to fulfill their part.

Additionally, Paul gives three reasons for universal subjection: (1) judgment by God if there are violations,[491] (2) government is designed to be an instrument of God's justice in dealing with good and evil,[492] (3) for conscience's sake[493] – presumably so that believers would not be seared in their consciences and find difficulty in decision making in other areas of life. Paul states the principle in terms of specific expression: "render to all what is due."[494] He adds four examples: tax, custom, fear, and honor,[495] reminding the reader that the only allowable continuously unpaid debt is that of love. That debt is never paid off and must always continue being paid. Taxes may

---

[486] Romans 13:1.
[487] Cf. 13:1 and 13:3.
[488] 13:3.
[489] 13:4.
[490] E.g., Ephesians 5:22-6:9,
[491] Romans 13:2.
[492] 13:3-4.
[493] 13:5.
[494] 13:7.
[495] 13:7.

be fulfilled when due, leaving no current balance due. Love, on the other hand, is always due. Thus subjection is to be accompanied by love.

Peter restates the universal subjection mandate,[496] similarly presenting the ideal situation: those governing are to be treated *as* sent by God.[497] The device Peter uses here (the Greek comparative *hos*) is the same he uses in 3:7 to show that the husband is to be considerate, living with his wife in an understanding way *as* with a weaker vessel. Peter is not calling the woman a weaker vessel, just saying the husband is to have that level of consideration for her – as if she was – to never have an unaware moment. In the same way, the posture of the governed is to give leadership the benefit of the doubt that the leaders themselves are sent by God. Importantly, Peter is not making the statement that *they are* sent by God, just that the governed should treat them that way.

Besides these two contexts, there are other brief NT passages discussing the believer's socio-political relationships. Jesus prescribes paying taxes in order to avoid offending the one to whom the tax is due.[498] He also acknowledges that some things are within the jurisdiction of Caesar, and should be treated that way.[499] But before making those statements, Jesus presented the important tenet that one cannot serve two masters, because inevitably their interests will conflict.[500] While He presented the axiom in the context of challenging His

---

[496] 1 Peter 2:13-14.
[497] 2:14.
[498] Matthew 17:24-27.
[499] 22:15-22.
[500] 7:24.

listeners to seek His kingdom rather than temporal wealth and reward, this principle is vital also for socio-political engagement.

Elsewhere Paul encourages believers to pray for those in authority, that they will lead well and that they will come to the knowledge of the truth.[501] In his instruction to Titus, Paul adds that believers should be subject, obedient, and ready for every good deed. They should avoid dissensions, reflecting the kindness of God.[502] Paul and the writer of Hebrews both encourage believers that being at peace with others and walking in unity are expected and reflective of their nature.[503]

These passages all share in common the stating of the ideal in socio-political relationships. There is no discussion of how to proceed when there is failure, division, or disunity. For that guidance we look to some of the historical accounts that model how one puts into practice the principles described in Scripture even when the other party is uncooperative.

DEALING WITH FAILURE, DIVISION, AND DISUNITY

Responding to Failures in Leadership

In Acts 1:8 Jesus commissioned Peter and the other apostles to be His witnesses, proclaiming His message throughout the world. But it didn't take long for opposition to form. After Peter and John healed a man and proclaimed the good news of Jesus,[504] the priests, temple leaders, and Sadducees had Peter and John arrested and put in jail.[505] At the

---

[501] 1 Timothy 2:1-4.
[502] Titus 3:1-11.
[503] Romans 12:17-18, Ephesians 4:1-3, Hebrews 12:14.
[504] Acts 3.
[505] 4:1-3.

public trial, again, Peter spoke up explaining the gospel of Jesus the Christ. Again, the opposition was disturbed.[506] This time the leaders gave Peter and John specific instruction that "they were not to speak or teach at all in the name of Jesus."[507] The response was remarkable: "Whether it is right in the sight of God to give heed to you rather than to God, you be the judge; for we cannot stop speaking about what we have seen and heard."[508] Peter and John recognized that the judgment in this situation belonged to the leaders, and they recognized that while the instructions they had been given were contradictory (Jesus had told them to speak of Him, the leaders were telling Peter and John not to speak of Jesus), they must obey God rather than man. As the apostles continued to proclaim Jesus, they were soon arrested again. The high priest reminded them of the instructions they had disobeyed.[509] They responded directly, "We must obey God rather than men."[510] They were whipped, released, and given the commandment again to stop speaking of this Jesus.[511] Of course, they continued speaking of Jesus,[512] and it is notable that they rejoiced that God had counted them worthy to suffer for Christ.[513]

This episode illustrates several important nuances of how believers should engage with government and each other. The apostles recognized the jurisdiction and authority of the leaders and subjected themselves to the consequences of their actions.

---

[506] 4:4-17.
[507] 4:18.
[508] 4:19-20.
[509] 5:27-28.
[510] 5:29.
[511] 5:40.
[512] 5:42.
[513] 5:41.

The only area that they disobeyed was in that which was directly contradictory to what God had already told them. They showed that there is an order of priority in serving God over humanity, because one can't serve two masters if the instructions conflict. These men illustrated that if civil disobedience is Biblically justified and engaged, there should still be subjection to the authorities, to their processes, and a willingness to receive the consequences.

The prioritization of God's direction over humanity's was not simply a church-age concept. Daniel modeled civil disobedience in Daniel 6, when leaders who were jealous of Daniel manipulated the king to enact a law that forbid prayer to anyone but the king.[514] Knowing that he would be breaking the new law, Daniel continued to pray to God in the manner he had previously.[515] Daniel submitted himself to the consequences of being put in the den of lions – he didn't flee or try to hide. Daniel did proclaim his innocence both before God and the king.[516] He recognized that even though he had broken the law, he hadn't sinned against the king.

In this instance God delivered Daniel, but of course we know He doesn't always allow the consequences to pass. But He did so in at least one other instance, when Shadrach, Meshach, and Abed-nego were told they had to bow down to worship Nebuchadnezzar's golden image and they refused.[517] The edict directly contradicted God's revealed law for Israel.[518] The three disobeyed Nebuchadnezzar's ungodly law and accepted the

---

[514] Daniel 6:4-9.
[515] 6:10.
[516] 6:22.
[517] 3:1-30.
[518] Exodus 20:3-4.

consequences, knowing that God was not obligated to deliver them.[519]

It wasn't just men who made the choices to obey God rather than humanity. Two Hebrew midwives named Shiphrah and Puah provide the *first* Biblical instances of appropriate civil disobedience.[520] Pharaoh gave them orders to kill newborn Hebrew males.[521] But because Shiphrah and Puah feared God they disobeyed the king's instruction,[522] and it appears they misled Pharaoh to make him think the women would give birth before the midwives arrived.[523] (Either the statement was true, it would have been because of the midwives' actions in some way, and they were manipulating in some way to ensure the statement would be true, or the statement was not true and they simply lied to protect the children and their families.) Presumably they understood the principle that Moses would later commit to writing in Genesis 9: that all human life is sacred because of the image of God. As He would do later with Shadrach, Meshach, Abed-Nego, and Daniel, God blessed these women because of their prioritization of God.

In all of these instances, the instructions disobeyed were failures not on the part of the governed, but on the part of the governors. These leaders enacted laws that were unrighteous, being in direct contradiction to what God had revealed and instructed. There was no subjectivity in these decisions. They were forced to follow God or follow human leaders. They couldn't

---

[519] Daniel 3:17-18.
[520] Exodus 1.
[521] 1:16.
[522] 1:17.
[523] 1:19.

do both. And in each of these cases, it appears there was gracious and respectful interaction with subjection in every other way.

It is worth noting that we have no Biblical examples of righteous persons disobeying authorities on any other grounds than direct contradiction to God's revealed word.[524] These Biblical examples of civil disobedience don't provide a license to disregard governance that is simply disagreeable. These examples are provided for much more serious circumstances.

Responding to Division and Disunity

As many moral problems as had existed in the church at Corinth, the first one addressed in Paul's letters to the Corinthians was the lack of unity among the people.[525] After extensive discussion of the problem and its implications, Paul prescribes a very straightforward solution: stop making judgments that are the Lord's jurisdiction and which require one to go beyond what is written.[526] Judging in this way promulgates subjectivity and leads to arrogance, because the subjective critics are elevating themselves over those they are judging.

In Paul's Letter to the Ephesians he explains that the unity of believers is rooted in grace,[527] and that believers should be diligent to preserve that unity.[528] He outlines several key components of that ongoing preservation: not walking in

---

[524] In the case of the Hebrew midwives, their actions took place before Genesis 8-9 was written by Moses, but of course the events of Genesis 8-9 had already taken place. It would have been highly probably that they would have been aware through the meticulous oral passing down of their people's history.

[525] 1 Corinthians 1:10.

[526] 4:5-6.

[527] Ephesians 4:7.

[528] 4:3.

accordance with the old nature but rather in the new,[529] considerate conduct that includes speaking truth, not living in anger, not stealing but sharing instead, speaking in an edifying way, and being kind, tenderhearted, and forgiving.[530] These are all necessary for believers to walk in a manner worthy of the calling with which they have been called and to preserve the unity that god has already provided.

Another crucial element of that continual expression of preservation is believers being subject to one another in the fear of Christ.[531] That mutual subjection undergirds every major familial and societal relationship a believer may encounter.[532] Submission is not just for the governed toward their governors, but of one brother and sister to another. The posture of the believer, again, is not one of asserting their rights and freedoms against one another, but rather in demonstrating Christlikeness in humility of mind and subjection to one another. Jesus' example of humility and sacrifice illustrates the kind of thinking we should have as we engage with each other.[533]

EXPRESSIONS OF GRACE IN POLITICAL ENGAGEMENT

Galatians 5:22-23 provides a list of the fruit the Spirit bears in us when we are walking in Him. Paul observers that "against such things there is no law." Paul is speaking ontologically here, not representatively. He is speaking of the concept of law – or *good* law, that no decent law would or could

---

[529] 4:17-24.
[530] 4:25-32.
[531] 5:21.
[532] E.g., 5:22-6:9.
[533] Philippians 2:1-11.

prohibit these characteristics. Such prohibition would be nonsensical. The problem we encounter, however, is that increasingly the world system seeks to eradicate any trace of the God it rejects, including the evidence of Him that His fruit in us provides. Sometimes socio-political differences can be attributed to the fact that the ongoing process of eradication is not necessarily obvious to many, and the progressive movement to that end can capture even the well-intentioned in its vortex. For times like these, Jude's exhortation is as apropos as ever: "...have mercy on some who are doubting; save others snatching them out of the fire; and on some have mercy with fear, hating even the garment polluted by the flesh."[534] The goal is not managing political principles and differences. The stakes are much higher than that. But because we are in a world where there are socio-political interactions and implications, we do need to be able to address how to practice Jude's kind of compassion in every area of the Christian life. So, what does that look like in political matters?

Considering these instructions and examples, we need to understand how to apply grace in our contemporary political engagement. In the United States, Christians live in a society governed by a Constitution, which is designed to guarantee the rights acknowledged by the Declaration of Independence – the unalienable right to life, liberty, and the pursuit of happiness because all men are created equal by their Creator. The American system of government allows its citizens perhaps a greater amount of freedom and recourse when those freedoms are violated than in any other contemporary or historical system of human led government. But governments change. And not

---

[534] Jude 1:22-23.

every place in which Christians live offers the same freedoms and recognition of rights. It is important, then, for us to ground our understanding of how to engage in socio-political matters not on tenuous and mutable governmental structures. Instead, we need to Biblically ground our understanding of how to engage socio-politically. When our bases are Biblical, we do not manage by the exceptional cases. Instead, we are able to confidently understand principles that can apply and be expressed in any setting. From the Biblical examples we have examined in this chapter, there are at least six applications or expressions of grace for how we engage with others in socio-political contexts:

1. Biblical Focus and Discernment – our judgments ought to be Biblically grounded. What other foundation is so reliable? Our experience deceives us, our reason betrays us, and our hearts are desperately sick. The one who builds his understanding on and applies well the word of God will have a foundation that will hold up in the most severe of storms.[535]

2. Humility and Selflessness – when we pursue our own interests above those of others outside of Biblical parameters, we elevate ourselves and place ourselves in the position of oppressors. This is a direct violation of the instructions given to follow Christ's example of humility and selflessness in His sacrifice on our behalf.[536]

3. Respect – it is a simple (though perhaps not easy) prescription to honor all humanity.[537] When committed to that outcome (that all are honored) we have much less energy to focus on honoring ourselves above others. We

---

[535] Matthew 7:24-27.
[536] Philippians 2:1-11.
[537] 1 Peter 2:17.

are reminded that we are to do good to all humanity,[538] even if there are prioritizations for how to order that good.

4. Subjection – as a basic expression within every human relationship, we must understand how submission works, why it is so important, and how it is expressed in each distinct relationship.

5. Edifying Speech – in the context of moving away from malice and anger, the quality of the speech of believers is determined by whether or not it builds up others. Bad words are those words which do not build up.

6. Prayerfulness – praying for all who are in authority is not optional.[539] There are important reasons for this activity – so that we may be free to live tranquil lives of godliness and dignity. Generally, when we lift up someone in prayer, because that is an act of grace in itself, it is much easier to think and speak well of them. In so doing we are approaching their Heavenly Father on their behalf, and in doing that our own care for them is likely to increase.

It should be obvious by now that these principles all represent *love*, and *grace is simply love bestowed when undeserved*. Because when dealing with fallen humanity love is always undeserved, we need to recognize the necessity of grace in every interaction. Others need our grace, and we need that of others – because we have *His grace*. If there is to be any authentic conception of social justice, it must be rooted in a Biblical understanding of the grace of God for each of us and the responsibility we have of showing that grace to each other.

---

[538] Galatians 6:9-10.
[539] 1 Timothy 2:1-2.

Made in the USA
Columbia, SC
15 January 2022

54210179R00115